The English Railway Station

The English
Railway Station

Steven Parissien

ENGLISH HERITAGE

Published by English Heritage, The Engine House, Fire Fly Avenue, Swindon SN2 2EH
www.english-heritage.org.uk
English Heritage is the Government's lead body for the historic environment.

First published 2014
Reprinted 2015

ISBN 978 1 84802 236 2

Product code 51777

British Library Cataloguing in Publication data
A CIP catalogue record for this book is available from the British Library.

For more information about images from the English Heritage Archive, contact Archives Services Team, The Engine House, Fire Fly Avenue, Swindon SN2 2EH; telephone (01793) 414600.

Brought to publication by Jess Ward, Publishing, English Heritage.

Typeset in Charter 9.5/11.75 and 9.5/12.75

Edited by Sparks Publishing Services Ltd
Proofread by Kim Bishop
Indexed by Ann Hudson
Designed by Hybert Design, UK

Printed in Belgium by Deckers Snoeck.

Frontispiece
Thomas Prosser's magnificent trainshed at York. (OP25562)

P viii
G T Andrews's memorable medieval booking hall at Richmond, North Yorkshire. (OP01450)

CONTENTS

ACKNOWLEDGEMENTS

I would like to thank all those who have helped me with the ideas and research for this book. Special thanks must go to John Hudson and Robin Taylor of English Heritage Publishing, for commissioning this project, and to Andrew Holt and James Hulme for their assistance and invaluable railway wisdom.

Particular thanks must go to Dr Rachel Stewart, for her help, advice, enthusiasm and support even in the most trying and unlikely of contexts.

INTRODUCTION

Before 1980, the endless shelves of literature on the railways of Britain contained almost no books on the railway station. Those authors who did address the subject of railway buildings – pioneering individuals such as Christian Barman and David Lloyd – were often peripheral figures in the world of railway history. (Jack Simmons was a glowing exception to this rule; John Betjeman, though, was always regarded by railway buffs as more of a media figure.) Even the best-illustrated and most authoritative of railway studies contained precious few illustrations of stations – even though related subjects such as signal boxes and track layout were generally exhaustively covered both pictorially and in prose.

Such neglect of the railway station reflected the low esteem in which this most important and characterful of building types was regarded for much of the 20th century. British Rail and its successors were still demolishing historic station structures well into the 1980s, and voices raised in protest against this needless vandalism – by railway enthusiasts, by the new heritage railway companies and even by the established national amenity societies – were invariably regarded as irritating, anachronistic nuisances by both the railway industry and by central government. In the late 1980s, however, the balance began to shift – just in time to exert a strong influence on the post-privatisation companies which succeeded British Rail after 1993. The National Railway Heritage Trust of 1985 demonstrated that station conservation was a subject that government and industry were now taking seriously, while published studies such as Jeffrey Richards and John M MacKenzie's invaluable *The Railway Station* and Gordon Biddle's comprehensive *Great Railway Stations of Britain*, both of 1986, brought the subject of the British station to a mainstream general audience. The tide now turned in favour of the retention or conservation of railway buildings, as both passengers and railway operators realised how architecturally, commercially and socially valuable such historic station structures could prove in a contemporary world.

This book does not pretend to be an exhaustive history of the station – to find out more about this fascinating subject, please refer to the further reading list at the end – but serves as an introduction to the architectural development, the social significance and, in the last century, the dramatic fall and rise of the English railway station. (Since this book was commissioned by English Heritage, its focus has accordingly been kept to England.) Much more could undoubtedly be said, for example, about the shameful and unnecessary destruction after 1945 of so much of our built railway heritage – but for that I direct the interested reader to John Minnis's splendid and evocative *Britain's Lost Railways* of 2011. Instead, I hope that this book serves to remind both those who are not familiar with the history of England's stations, as well as those that are, of the magnificent railway heritage that we have by turns squandered and retained, and of the increasing significance and value of the railway station in a more environmentally aware age.

1

Genesis

'No one visits railway stations to look at architecture' pronounced railway writer James Scott in the *The Railway and Travel Monthly* of June 1911.[1] Looking at the stock of many railway centre bookshops today, this judgement may still seem to be borne out. Thankfully, the evidence of station sites the length and breadth of England suggests that, since the dramatic re-appreciation of the architectural and social worth of the railway station in recent years, the very opposite is true. And for good reason.

Railways stations were not always regarded as the despised symbols of a past age that they were during the 1950s and 1960s. At the height of the Railway Age of the 19th century, the French poet Théophile Gautier famously asserted that stations were 'cathedrals of the new humanity', while the novelist and polemicist Emile Zola declared that 'our artists must find the poetry of stations as their fathers found that of forests and rivers'. As early as 1850, indeed, the Irish scientist Dr Dionysus Lardner had written in his *Railway Economy* that 'It is impossible to regard the vast buildings and their dependencies ... without feelings of inexpressible astonishment at the magnitude of the capital and boldness of the enterprise.'[2] A century later Lardner was echoed by railway historian Gordon Biddle, who pronounced that 'the tremendous variety of station styles formed a microcosm of 19th-century building.'[3] Sadly, many of the buildings Biddle was to hymn in his groundbreaking book *Victorian Stations* of 1973 had, a decade later, succumbed to the dispiriting myopia of British Rail.

In the beginning

Neither the railway nor the railway station were, as is often thought, Victorian creations. What may be the oldest surviving 'true' station in Britain dates from the reign of King George III: a handsome, three-bay, pedimented brick

structure in Mitcham, Surrey, now in the residential use its domesticated design always suggested (Fig 1.1). Some theories suggest the station was actually built for the horse-drawn Surrey Iron Railway in 1803; alternatively, its large, arched carriage entrance may suggest it was simply an existing inn which was subsequently harnessed by the steam-operated Wimbledon and Croydon Railway when it arrived in Mitcham in 1855 – the original horse-drawn railway having foundered nine years earlier. Even if Mitcham Station is discounted, the first railway in Britain (and, indeed, the entire world) intended for the transport of both goods and passengers, with vehicles hauled by steam-powered locomotives – the Stockton and Darlington Railway (S&DR) – was authorised by parliament in 1821, the year of King George IV's coronation.

When the S&DR opened for passenger business on 27 September 1825, fares were paid at a brick line-side house at 48 Bridge Street,

Fig 1.1
Mitcham, Surrey: principal elevation. (BB048981)

Fig 1.2
48 Bridge Street, Stockton.
(AA97/01838)

Stockton – a building which still survives, albeit in private ownership (Fig 1.2). The S&DR did not consider opening formal, passenger-focused stations to be a major priority in their early years. There never was a proper station at Stockton, while at the other end of the line the first passengers alighted at Darlington at a barely marked point near the Great North Road. From 1833, Darlington passengers were at least able to exploit the shelter of a new, line-side warehouse; six years later, the S&DR built another shed, this time on the west side of the Great North Road, on top of which the first

Fig 1.3
The ticket office at
Darlington North Road in
the 1950s.
(OP01418)

purpose-built station was finally constructed in 1842. (In 1856 the Great North Road was straightened at this point, leaving the new station standing, rather forlornly, some distance from the main road.) Inexplicably, given their importance in the history of the world's railways, during the 1960s both line and station were under threat (Fig 1.3); thankfully, today the sedately classical, six-bay main building enjoys a Grade II* listing on account of its historic importance, lies at the heart of a World Heritage Site and, appropriately, houses a railway museum. As an added bonus, trains (on the local service to Bishop's Auckland) do actually still stop there.

The S&DR's initiative was swiftly followed up all over England. The Canterbury and Whitstable Railway was authorised by Parliament in 1825 and opened on 3 May 1830 (a month before George IV's death). The Liverpool and Manchester Railway (L&MR) was authorised in 1826, and opened in dramatic circumstances on 15 September 1830. The Newcastle and Carlisle Railway was sanctioned on 22 May 1829, although it only opened to passengers on 9 March 1835. And what started life as the Grand Junction Railway, a route which had originally been proposed by John Rennie and George Stephenson back in 1823 but which was only given parliamentary approval in an Act of 1833, finally opened in 1838 as the London and Birmingham Railway (L&BR).

Its pivotal role as the world's first public railway notwithstanding, the S&DR did not build the world's first purpose-built, permanent railway station. This appeared in 1830, when the S&DR was still expecting its passengers to mount or alight from its exceedingly basic carriages with no architectural assistance. As Yale University's legendary architectural historian Professor Carroll Meeks wrote, it was the L&MR's Crown Street terminus in Edge Hill, to the east of Liverpool's city centre, which ...

embodied the basic features of the modern station in embryo. The passenger preparing to depart from Liverpool arrived by carriage or omnibus at a vehicle court – foreshadowing the covered driveway of later stations ... On entering the building he found himself in a room which combined the function of tickets selling and waiting, as in the great concourse of today's terminals [Meeks was writing in the mid-1950s]. From the waiting-room he passed onto the platform and into his carriage under the cover of a train-shed, the degree of protection as greater than it is in many recent stations.[4]

Liverpool Crown Street's commission reflected the early railways' predilection for employing a well-known, established architect to create a building which was, for the actual or putative passenger, both solidly familiar and warmly reassuring. Crown Street (Fig 1.4) was designed by John Foster, who added it onto the end of an existing, three-storey sandstone house of 1808 and phrased it in a robust and simple late-Georgian classical idiom, even providing it with a ground floor clad in that very domestic (and rather old-fashioned) stone finish of vermiculated rustication. From the street, the new station thus looked like any other aspirational, middle-class townhouse. Separate entrances for first- and second-class passengers were created within the economical, four-bay façade, and a hipped-roof platform canopy on slender iron columns was later added to the east.

John Foster (c 1787–1846) was presumably chosen by the L&MR as he had already built up a sizeable reputation in the city as a safe pair of classical hands. He had studied under Jeffry Wyatville, the architect of Windsor Castle and a large number of prestigious country houses, and had studied abroad in Greece in the company of the architect C R Cockerell, who subsequently and slightingly described Foster as 'a most amusing youth, but too idle to be anything more than a dinner companion'.[5] Cockerell was proved wrong. In 1824, Foster succeeded his father as Architect to the Corporation of Liverpool, and at the same time was made Professor of Ancient and Modern Architecture of the Liverpool Academy of Arts. Thereafter he proceeded to populate the rapidly growing city with impressive neoclassical monuments, of which Crown Street Station was but a small foretaste.

In the event, Foster's Crown Street lasted only six years as Liverpool's principal railway terminus. In 1836, Lime Street Station was opened closer to the centre, and Crown Street Station was rebuilt to the northeast as Edge Hill Station. Foster's original Crown Street, however, survived as a goods station until 1975.

At the eastern end of the L&MR, Manchester's far humbler Liverpool Road terminus – effectively little more than a stuccoed house fronting a pitched awning and meagre platform – ironically survived a little longer than Foster's Crown Street. In 1844, however, rail services were transferred from Liverpool Road to the new, more centrally located Victoria Station. The handsome, stone-fronted building still survives as the world's oldest surviving terminus

Railways in the 'Thirties'.

station, as part of Manchester's Museum of Science and Industry; since 1975 the building has also doubled as a location for Granada TV's evergreen soap opera *Coronation Street*. With hideous irony, though, one of the world's oldest railway stations is currently threatened by a projected railway development.

Most of the early railway stations were, as historians Jeffrey Richards and John Mackenzie have noted, 'an assortment of sheds, huts and barns, invariably scruffy, draughty and uncomfortable',[6] which were intended to serve both passenger and freight. As we have seen at Darlington, passengers were generally expected to climb up into trains from the lineside. Both termini of the new Leeds and Selby Railway of 1834, for example, comprised simple wooden sheds, with wooden trussed roofs supported internally on cast-iron columns, with no platform provided for passengers. Indeed, the earliest railways were not actually very interested in passengers: goods traffic was, the railway companies assumed, always going to remain their principal business, while carrying people would remain, they predicted, merely a minor sideline. As designer Christian Barman noted in 1950:

there [was] always a temporary look about these simple wooden shelters; it is as if those who built them knew they were dealing with an invention whose full development was certain to be so tremendous that it was useless for them to try to forecast what it would be like.[7]

By the mid-1830s, however, it was clear to the more perceptive companies that it might, after all, be worth bothering with what could well prove a highly lucrative market.

Fig 1.4
Liverpool Crown Street soon after opening in 1830. (RO/04628/001)

A new building type

The first permanent stations built in stone or brick were based on the stylistic precepts of domestic architecture. This was not just because this was a building type with which most architects were most familiar; it was also, as we have noted, to reassure the first passengers that the railway was safe and reassuring – just like home – and not dangerous or frightening. This was, after all, an important objective in the early years of the railways, a time when many passengers lost their lives in appalling and well-publicised accidents. No matter that, by 1851, the chance of a passenger being killed on the railways was in actuality over 420,000 to 1; the frequency with which newspaper reports gleefully recounted, in ghoulish detail, tales of demolished platforms, collapsing bridges, train fires and head-on collisions convinced many otherwise. New railway stations had to impart reassurance, confidence and calmness. For example, at Newark Castle, an early stone station built by the Midland Railway in 1846

Fig 1.5 (below)
Newark Castle,
Nottinghamshire, 1846.
(BB94/15098)

Fig 1.6 (bottom)
Ashby-de-la-Zouch,
Leicestershire, 1849.
(RO/02522/001)

(Fig 1.5), pilasters and a heavy stone entablature were applied to a projecting, three-bay entrance to give this single-storey edifice the assurance of grandeur, longevity and stability. The same principle was used at the Midland's station at Ashby-de-la-Zouch of 1849 (Fig 1.6), where Greek Doric columns in antis flanked an imposing entrance which resembled a grand chapel or Freemasons' hall.

The key components of the railway station were broadly the same from 1835 to 2014: platforms abutting the railway tracks, often covered by an overall trainshed or, at least, by sheltered platform canopies; and the offices and accommodation – which, in the case of larger branch or main-line termini, were increasingly housed in a building placed across the end of the tracks (which Meeks termed the 'head-building'). By 1900, the island platform, sited between tracks and linked to a station entrance by a bridge or tunnel, had become common, given that it saved the railway companies considerable amounts of money in terms of both roadside buildings and staff. The cash-strapped Great Central Railway (GCR) built a number of these island stations during the course of its late voyage towards London.

Early carriages had step-boards, like road carriages, so the platforms were low; but by 1900 platforms had generally risen to the level of the carriage itself. Some stations linked separated platforms by footbridge or subway; other – generally more rural – stations relied on a precarious foot crossing at grade, in order to save money.

In 1840, the surveyor-engineer Francis Whishaw published what turned out to be a rather premature guide: *Railways of Great Britain and Ireland*. Whishaw, born in 1804, had worked under George Stephenson surveying the Manchester and Leeds Railway in 1835; he was also the first professional secretary for the Society of Arts from 1843 to 1845, during which time he helped to promote the cause of what became the Great Exhibition of 1851. His 1845 demonstration of gutta-percha – a durable, natural latex derived from tree sap – encouraged Anglo-German engineer William Siemens to use it for insulating cables. His *Railways of Great Britain and Ireland* was a comprehensive survey of what had been built by the railways up until that point. Whishaw strongly implied that this mode of travel was no mere fad, and that railways, and railway stations, were very much here to stay.

Fig 1.7
Sir William Tite's splendid
Carlisle Citadel Station,
opened in 1847.
(DP066289)

It was not initially assumed, though, that each railway company would always have its own dedicated station. The directors of the Great Western Railway (GWR) originally approached the rival L&BR with a proposal that the two companies share the latter's new London terminus at Euston. Indeed, the provision of space for the GWR, it has been suggested, may have partly accounted for Euston's subsequent illogical, lopsided plan. A separate new station at Paddington was only contemplated when the L&BR persistently refused to heed the GWR's pleas. In a similar vein, the London and North Western Railway (LNWR), which had absorbed the L&BR in 1846 – largely in response to the GWR's perceived empire-building, now refused to let the GWR use their New Street terminus at Birmingham. After numerous attempts to cajole and persuade, the GWR finally gave up and, in 1852, built its own city-centre station at Snow Hill. Even then, the building at Snow Hill was a decidedly half-hearted wooden structure – as if the company was patiently waiting for the LNWR to see reason and change its mind. It was only in 1906 that the GWR began to build a truly permanent station wholly worthy of the now-wealthy city of Birmingham.

In most cases, British cities eschewed the type of large, single, multi-company station popular in the USA. Most American cities had the space in which to re-route railway lines and resite termini, and few valuable buildings or established industrial concerns to get in the way. In authoritarian states like the post-1870 German Reich, a strong, centralised political will helped to override local vested interests. In Britain, however, civic pride and commercial influence were enviably robust, and what the Americans called the 'union' station (which the British called 'joint station') was actually rare.

A few union stations were built in England. Sir William Tite's magnificent Citadel Station at Carlisle, for example (Fig 1.7), was originally intended for seven railway companies: the Newcastle and Carlisle Railway (which arrived in the city as early as 1836), the Maryport and Carlisle, the Lancaster and Carlisle, the Caledonian, the Glasgow and South-Western, the Port Carlisle (taken over by the North British Railway in 1862) and the LNWR. When the Midland Railway arrived in the burgeoning city in 1876, via its spectacular if vastly expensive Settle–Carlisle line, it was not encouraged to build a separate station on a different site, in the usual muddled British way, but was happily accommodated within an enlarged Citadel Station. Similarly, at Bristol two years later, the existing Brunel and Fripp termini at Temple Meads were effectively replaced by a spacious 'joint' station by M D Wyatt – a task admittedly made easier by the fact that all of Temple Meads' lines were owned by one company: the GWR. However, Carlisle and Bristol were exceptions. In the nation's capital, railways were not even allowed to cross the River Thames until 1860. And, as late as the 1890s, Sir Edward Watkin's GCR extension to London avoided existing railway hubs, either due to Watkin's hubris or to the stubborn opposition of the existing railways, or to a combination of both, and built its own stations at major centres such as Nottingham, Leicester and Rugby. Derided for the next 60 years as unnecessary and wasteful irrelevancies, these GCR stations were all to fall to Beeching's axe in the 1960s.

The grand, purpose-built railway stations of the 1830s and 1840s were regional attractions, drawing thousands of visitors and many admiring comments. They were intended to impress shareholders with the solidity and profitability of the company, and travellers with safety, reliability and success. They also, it was quickly realised, provided exciting new markets for quick-witted retailers to plumb. Thus, in 1848, the newsvending concern WH Smith was granted the exclusive right to sell books and newspapers on the London to Birmingham line of the LNWR. Its first bookstall was erected at Euston in 1848, and by 1851 it was operating news-stands across the LNWR's network. From 1863, WH Smith was equipping all the principal railways with bookstalls – a monopoly which they exercised until 1905. Not that the books sold by WH Smith and their smaller rivals were necessarily high-minded; critics coined the pejorative term 'railway novel' to typify the kind of trashy, melodramatic book now available at the station.

Railway time

The railway station was also increasingly identified by local communities as the point at which time was defined and calibrated. The standardised time shown on the station clock underlined the national nature of the railways and the consequent shrinking of Britain. Local time, even if it had differed substantially from that of the capital (for example, the time at Barrow was, in pre-railway days, 13 minutes behind that of London), thanks to the railway, now rapidly became meaningless and unhelpful. The GWR was the first railway to standardise its timetable to London's Greenwich Mean Time (GMT) – now popularly known as 'railway time' – in November 1840. By 1847, the Railway Clearing House – which George Hudson had set up five years earlier to coordinate the distribution of revenue between railway companies – decreed that GMT should be adopted at all stations as soon as the General Post Office had permitted it. By 1855, 95 per cent of British towns and cities had transferred to GMT. Some stationmasters stubbornly refused to alter their station clocks away from traditional, local time, but in 1880 it became a legal requirement.

By 1850, locals were also using the station not just to check the correct time but also to send messages. In 1839, the GWR opened the world's first railway telegraph line between Paddington and West Drayton and, by 1868, 21,751 miles of line in the UK were covered by telegraph. In 1884 the Midland Railway alone sent five million telegrams on behalf of the public. Thus was the station made the centre of local communications.

Other services soon appeared at local stations. Left luggage offices, for example, were introduced from 1840. Around the same time the first lost property offices were installed at principal termini. Lavatories came later – far too late for many passengers' convenience. By 1895, the sanitation entrepreneur George Jennings, who had provided public conveniences for the Great Exhibition of 1851, was supplying 30 railway companies with his tile-clad and marble-provisioned facilities. However, male-run railway companies have always seemed to be lagging behind female demand. As late as 2013 the gleaming new terminus at St Pancras International belatedly rebuilt its principal under-concourse toilets so that women arriving at this flagship station would not have to endure interminable queues to access the main ladies' lavatory.

Stations soon had to incorporate facilities – and often accommodation, too – for the staff as well as for the passengers. From 1840, most of the larger stations began to incorporate a small house for the stationmaster – or, at smaller, rural stations, for the station clerk. However, as the railways became centralised following the enforced 'Grouping' of 1923 – when most of Britain's railways were effectively nationalised into four large regional companies: the GWR (the only railway to retain its pre-grouping identity); the Southern; the London, Midland and Scottish (LMS); and the London and North Eastern Railway (LNER) – so stationmasters and station clerks began to become superfluous, particularly at the lesser stops. This process accelerated when the railway was completely nationalised in 1948, after which stationmasters across the country were laid off and their houses emptied. Thankfully, today, these well-built dwellings often survive as private homes, even when the railway (or even the station) they were built to serve has disappeared.

The stationmaster was not always the only inhabitant of the station. Station dogs and cats were soon common, with a select few of the dog population being trained to collect money from the public for charity. Birmingham Snow Hill's Edwardian station dog, 'Dash', raised on average an astonishing 15 shillings a week from passing passengers. The most famous station pet, however, was Slough's 'Station Jim', who wandered the platforms in harness from 1894 till his death two years later with a charity box strapped to his back, collecting for the widows and orphans of GWR personnel. Jim was taught to bark whenever he received a coin, could beg

on his hind legs, and if anyone deposited a lighted cigarette on the platform he would stub it out with his paw – and with a growl. He occasionally got onto a paused train to travel about the GWR network – the furthest he ever reached was Leamington – but was always returned to Slough. Here he remains today, stuffed and exhibited in a glass case on Platform 5.

Class consciousness

Early stations, from Liverpool Crown Street onwards, also increasingly sought to maintain Victorian society's rigid class divisions. Not only did Brunel's Temple Meads terminus at Bristol (Fig 1.8) sensibly seek to separate outgoing from incoming passengers; it also provided separate staircases for first- and second-class passengers. Later stations even offered different lavatories, refreshment rooms and waiting rooms for the separate classes, in order to maintain a strict social segregation.

Initially, attempts to separate both classes and types of passenger were hampered by the simplistic arrangement of the first stations. Temple Meads, for example, was a variant of a station type that found favour in the early years

Fig 1.8
Brunel's original terminus at Bristol Temple Meads, opened in 1840. (OP25556)

of railways: the one-sided station. It was so large that it could provide both an arrival and a departure platform at each side; however, this disposition necessitated the complex shunting of locomotives and carriages. Philip Hardwick's Euston and Lewis Cubitt's King's Cross, too, were originally planned with one arrivals platform and one departures platform. The recent removal of the modern apron at King's Cross effectively returns the station to a plan reminiscent of its original layout – even though it is now served by a vast new concourse to the west. Yet other large stations of the time, such as Francis Thompson's Derby of 1839–41, essentially comprised one long platform – sometimes stretching to over 304m (1,000ft) – at which trains both arrived and departed. This was convenient for passengers, whose walk to the station buildings (and the exit), or to change trains, was minimal and at grade. However, as the 1840s progressed, more railway traffic meant that one-sided platforms soon became hopelessly congested. David Mocatta's Brighton of 1840–1 pointed the way forward for larger termini: all passengers entered and arrived via a concourse at the south end of multiple platforms, and all used the head-building at its southern end. The last purpose-built, one-sided station was John Dobson's Newcastle Central, opened by Queen Victoria in 1850; subsequently, though, island platforms were added to the south of Dobson's single platform. Cambridge survived as a one-sided station – albeit with bay platforms at the south end of its exceedingly long, 470m (1,542ft) platform – from its creation in 1845 until 2011, when an island platform was finally added on the eastern half of the site.

The adaptation of the station plan to keep different classes of passengers separate was similarly doomed to failure once railway traffic increased. As early as 1858, railway engineer Robert Jacomb Hood admitted that the struggle to keep the classes apart had not been successful. Thereafter, first-class passengers could only take refuge from the *hoi polloi* in designated waiting rooms and, in the larger stations, in single-class refreshment rooms. Only royalty, it was felt, had earned station entrances that were architecturally separate.

A stable future

British stations rarely employed the Continental and American answer to station congestion, by which a long bridge or tunnel, either linked to a stand-alone building incorporating the concourse and offices or serving as the concourse itself, stretched over or under a series of island platforms. Most British stations simply provided footbridges to cross from platform to platform – not a helpful solution for disabled or elderly passengers. Brunel ingeniously provided retractable drawbridges to bridge the tracks at grade, which were stored under the platforms when not in use; however, these proved clumsy and labour-intensive in practice, and were soon abandoned.

As the concept of railways became more familiar, so the architecture of stations, like that of banks, became ever more grandiose and ostentatious, as if to assure passengers of the rock-like fiscal stability of this innovative enterprise. This trend was particularly necessary after the great railway collapse of the late 1840s, which made the whole railway industry seem suddenly vulnerable. As Michael Freeman has noted, 'It was the architect's task to counter the anxieties and terrors that characterized many of the first public reactions to the steam railway'.[8] To that end, architects used familiar architectural styles for the public face of the station. Iron and glass were used to create the internal trainshed but, in the early years, familiar motifs, materials and masses were employed in the principal offices so as not to, sometimes quite literally, frighten the horses. The widespread use of the comfortable 'Tudorbethan' style for stations during the 1840s and 1850s neatly conveyed domesticity and politeness – qualities Christian Barman later summarised as 'manners'. The particular personality of each Tudoresque station also implied a degree of individuality, countering John Ruskin's objection that railway passengers were no longer real travellers but human parcels.

The proclaimed need to develop a distinctive railway style of architecture, and to move away from comfy Tudor or domestic classicism, was one that taxed architectural critics throughout the 1840s and 1850s. Ruskin himself, in his *Seven Lamps of Architecture* of 1849 – one of the most influential architectural books of the 19th century – advised that 'railroad architecture has, or would have, a dignity of its own if it were only left to its work. You would not put rings on the fingers of a smith at his anvil'.[9] Following Ruskin, many railway architects sought to lend decorum and grandeur to a means of transport which was, in the eyes of many, fraught with danger and risk. Thus station buildings needed

to be simultaneously solid and spectacular – whether their model was Hardwick's giant portico at Euston, Brunel's imposing Tudor palace at Bristol or Cubitt's Brobdingnagian brick arches at King's Cross. The collapse of George Hudson's house of cards in 1849 seemed to confirm to many observers that the whole railway business was merely a vehicle for irresponsible speculation, and would prove a temporary fad.

In the early years of the station, the classical portico was frequently enlisted to provide the requisite Ruskinian dignity. J P Pritchett's Huddersfield of 1847 (Fig 1.9), built for the Huddersfield and Manchester and the Manchester and Leeds Railways, is perhaps the outstanding English regional station of the early railway years. Its pedimented Corinthian portico fronted a central block with Corinthian pilasters and pedimented side elevations (the sort of detail that later stations would eschew), linked to pedimented pavilions by long, single-storey colonnades. The result resembled the large, mid-Georgian Yorkshire country house Wentworth Woodhouse – unsurprisingly, since Pritchett had been architect to the Earls Fitzwilliam, owners of Wentworth Woodhouse, for some years. Pritchett's original plan, as commissioned by the wealthy Ramsden family who owned much of Huddersfield, was to use the imposing classical station as the centrepiece for a new civic centre: St George's Square. Disappointingly, Pritchett's projected town hall was never built – a town hall of much lesser architectural weight was eventually built on a

different site in 1878–81. Yet his magnificent station still dominates the town centre, terminating the vista up Northumberland Street in heroic fashion.

Further north, Monkwearmouth Station (Fig 1.10), designed by local architect Thomas Moore in 1848, which now houses a small railway museum, began life as the terminus of the Brandling Junction branch of the York and Newcastle Railway, which in 1854 was absorbed into the North Eastern Railway (NER). A grand, tetrastyle Ionic portico was flanked by wings

Fig 1.9
J P Pritchett's Huddersfield Station of 1847.
(BB98/24433)

Fig 1.10
The portico of Thomas Moore's Monkwearmouth of 1848.
(OP01443)

incorporating Greek Doric columns and Tuscan pilasters; the result was a strikingly handsome classical civic building which resonated with dignity and permanence.

The man behind the impressive stone façade of Monkwearmouth was both the local MP and the chairman – indeed the creator – of the York and Newcastle Railway. He was also about to become the most notorious figure in the early history of the railways. By the 1830s George Hudson (1800–71), the fifth son of a farmer from Yorkshire's East Riding, had progressed from running a drapery business in York to establishing a city bank and promoting a railway line from York to Leeds. The latter soon evolved into the York and North Midland Railway (engineered by George Stephenson), and subsequently into a network of railways across Yorkshire, County Durham and Northumberland. Elected MP for Sunderland in 1845 (a seat he tenaciously held onto until 1859) and, by 1845, vastly wealthy, he seemed the embodiment of the Railway Age and was lauded in the press as the 'Railway King'. However, in 1849 (barely a year after Monkwearmouth had opened), it was revealed that Hudson's railway empire was built on the quicksands of bribed MPs, shareholder dividends paid from capital, and large-scale personal embezzlement. Those who had always regarded the expansion of the railways with grave mistrust were seemingly vindicated (Thomas Carlyle called Hudson a 'big swollen gambler'). In the subsequent financial panic, hundreds of shareholders were ruined. Hudson, meanwhile, was forced to resign all of his numerous railway directorships, and spent much of the rest of his life in self-imposed exile in France. He finally returned to York in 1865, only to find himself summarily imprisoned in York Castle for fraud.

A roof overhead

Hudson's fall, however, proved to be only a brief interruption to the seemingly inexorable expansion of the railway network. And, as stations proliferated and grew, railways recognised that passengers and – more importantly – freight both needed more than the simple, lean-to or cantilevered platform canopies that were originally provided for shelter. Overall, station roofs ensured that the goods brought by rail were not spoiled by inclement weather whilst being loaded or unloaded. They also, of course, kept passengers dry – and had the added architectural benefit of literally raising the station's civic profile.

The first Liverpool Lime Street, built by John Cunningham and engineer George Stephenson and provided with a classical façade of 1835–6 by John Foster, was the first major station to have an overall roof supported by internal iron framing. Its completion also made Liverpool the first city with a single central terminus – in contrast to its great Lancashire rival Manchester, which had three dislocated termini serving different lines. Cast-iron columns were arranged in the first supportive trainshed 'colonnade', while the wooden roof was glazed at the apex and in strips down the side.

Within six years, however, the original Lime Street needed to be rebuilt, and a new roof, designed by engineers Richard Turner and William Fairburn and provided with a daring single curved span, was erected in 1848–9. In the north-east, John and Benjamin Green had already built a triple-arched trainshed at North Shields, in 1839. Across the Pennines, the Preston and Wyre Railway termini at Lytham and Blackpool, both of 1846, each featured single-span trainsheds. The gifted railway architect, G T Andrews, widely used iron-trussed overall wooden roofs in his East Riding stations of the mid-1840s for the NER, while 1849 saw the completion of John Dobson's three, epically scaled, curved trainsheds, each 18.3m (60ft) wide, at Newcastle Central.

Glazing of these early roofs was rare but, by the 1850s, ridge-and-furrow glazing was being employed both for overall station roofs and for platform awnings. Joseph Paxton's Crystal Palace of 1851 showed how large iron-and-glass structures could be made that were both light and strong, and pointed the way ahead for trainshed design. At the same time, the rapid growth in railway traffic saw trainsheds grow ever wider – thanks to such engineering innovations as the elliptical, cast-iron crescent truss. Curved or arched trusses were, Victorian engineers rapidly discovered, stronger than traditional, triangular trusses, whose pointed apexes were invariably weak. This allowed for broader roof spans of the kind introduced by the innovative engineer E A Cowper at his trainshed at Birmingham New Street of 1854 (Fig 1.11), which Cowper had built by his own firm, Fox, Henderson & Company, who had recently been the contractors at Joseph Paxton's astonishing, iron-and-glass cathedral, Hyde Park's Crystal Palace.

Not all of the overall roofs built at the larger early stations were made or stabilised with iron. King's Cross, built by Lewis Cubitt for the Great Northern Railway (GNR) in 1850–2, was innovatory in many respects. The double-spanned trainshed was reflected in the station's simple brick elevation (Fig 1.12) – a feature introduced at François Duquesnay's Gare de l'Est in Paris of 1847, and which soon became a defining characteristic of larger continental stations. But Cubitt – best known until then as a bridge engineer and as the architect of the London terraces planned by his better-known elder brother, Thomas – intended his station to be large but starkly functional. 'The building will depend for its effect', he declared, 'on the largeness of some of the features, its fitness for its purpose and its characteristic expression

Fig 1.11
E A Cowper's magnificent trainshed of 1854 at Birmingham New Street, tragically lost to a combination of German bombs and civic vandalism. (RO/04003/031)

Fig 1.12
Cubitt's King's Cross pictured in c 1965. By 1972 the small porch had grown to a large, unsightly apron. (AA061597)

of that purpose.'[10] And his King's Cross stayed within the engineering boundaries with which he was familiar. Not for Cubitt the elevations of iron and glass of the contemporary Crystal Palace, nor the termini at Paddington, Birmingham New Street and Liverpool Lime Street. King's Cross's roof ribs were made not of iron but of laminated wood, each rib comprising 16 × 1½in (0.038m) boards bolted together and bound with an iron band. Nevertheless, by 1850, the wooden-ribbed trainshed at King's Cross was an old-fashioned rarity; some years later, Cubitt's laminated ribs were themselves replaced by iron equivalents.

Cubitt's King's Cross was unusual in that an engineer had designed both the trainshed and the head-building which incorporated the station facilities and offices. Most early termini preferred to employ an architect for the front-facing 'architecture' – Philip Hardwick at Euston, his son Philip Charles at Paddington – and an engineer to design the trainshed. This rigid division of labour continued through to St Pancras of 1865–73. At King's Cross (as at John Dobson's Newcastle Central), Cubitt acted as both – although his task was made vastly easier by the fact that the station's footprint did not incorporate a hotel: Cubitt's subsequent Great

Northern Hotel was an afterthought, built to moderate standards on a separate site to the north-west. In 1968 the pro-modernist architectural historian Sir John Summerson singled out Cubitt's King's Cross for praise on account of its 'acceptable union' of architecture and engineering, while lambasting later creations such as St Pancras for the total separation of functional and 'artistic' criteria – a separation of responsibility which the historian Robert Furneaux Jordan diagnosed in 1969 as 'schizophrenia'.

Notwithstanding the praise heaped on the functional simplicity of Cubitt's King's Cross during the 20th century, the larger Victorian stations that succeeded King's Cross invariably boasted overall roof spans of iron and glass, often resting on colonnades of cast-iron columns. And their roofs were getting wider and wider: the shed at Cowper's Birmingham New Street spanned 64.3m (211ft) in one leap, while Brunel's Paddington embraced 72.5m (238ft) in three spans. Yet, for all these marvellous achievements, the critics of the post-1945 era looked back at the Victorian age and lamented that, in hindsight, the structural possibilities offered by iron and glass had not been fully realised, and that architecture had continued to get in the way of engineering.

Fig 1.13
Ridge-and-furrow platform canopies at the Great Eastern's Coborn Road Station in East London of 1865.
(RO/22140/001)

In the face of such prejudice, it is rather surprising that, after 1945, many stations lost the overall roofs on which critics had lavished such praise. Most medium-sized stations had been provided with discrete canopies covering each platform; these, though, were also frequently sacrificed to the post-war passion for modernisation, rationalisation and a maintenance-free regime.

Grander platform canopies of the mid-19th century were often glazed using the ridge-and-furrow method, the resultant ridges creating an attractive row of gables – as at the GER's Coborn Road Station in the East End of London, of 1865 (Fig 1.13). On occasion the gables were provided with curved valances – as at the Lancashire and Yorkshire Railway's Burscough Junction in Lancashire, of 1849, whose gables were half-timbered in a domestic manner, and at the Midland Railway's impressive Kettering Station of 1857 (Fig 1.14), where

C H Driver's slender iron columns and large iron brackets, filled with exuberant floral decoration, supported the large but graceful ridge-and-furrow canopy which covered much of the island platform. Sadly, Coborn Road was closed and demolished as early as 1946. The splendid ironwork at Kettering, made by the local firm of Biddle & Co, still survives, despite enlargements of the station in 1879 and 1896 and the insensitive rationalisation of the 1970s – when, predictably, British Rail proposed to demolish much of Driver's virtuoso ironwork and to replace the glazed canopy with plastic sheeting. Kettering's local civic society strenuously opposed the proposals, and won; in the event, the 1857 canopy and its supports were sympathetically restored by Railtrack. The characterful platform canopy at Burscough Junction, though, was senselessly demolished in 1973, and crude plastic bus shelters installed in its place.

Fig 1.14
The delicate ironwork of C H Driver's platform canopies at Kettering, built for the Midland Railway in 1857.
(BB033018)

Fig 1.16 (opposite top)
Francis Thompson's
original, and much
celebrated, 'Tri Junct'
station at Derby,
unnecessarily demolished
over two decades.
(OP01425)

Fig 1.17 (opposite bottom)
Cubitt's dull and
workmanlike Great
Northern Hotel at King's
Cross of 1854. After the
Midland Grand opened
across the road in 1873 the
'Great Northern' looked even
more dowdy.
(BB009449)

The majority of small stations deemed worthy of platform shelters in the Victorian era were provided with cantilevered wooden canopies, supported on wooden or iron brackets. There were many variants of this pattern, though. Thus the LNWR's Gnosall of 1849 (closed in 1964) possessed no separate platform awnings but merely continued its wooden roof over the platform in one huge segmental arch, supported on large wooden brackets. By the later 1850s, many of these platform canopies were terminating in wooden valances, standardised to the approved company profile. The London, Brighton and South Coast Railway (LBSCR), for example, employed flat segmental arches along the plain valancing to create what Ian Nairn termed a 'loping' effect, though the 1882 rebuilding of the LBSCR's East Grinstead introduced a floral valance in the contemporary Aesthetic manner. The GER's valances, in contrast, were often finished in a suitably Tudoresque manner, reminiscent of the Elizabethan strapwork which featured in so many 16th- and 17th-century great houses in East Anglia.

A room for the night

Railway hotels, closely integrated with the station they served, were a uniquely British – or perhaps British-Imperial – phenomenon. G T Andrews was the first architect to incorporate a hotel into the station site, at York in 1838. At Euston in the following year, two undemonstrative, classical hotel blocks were built: the 'Victoria' to the west and the slightly superior 'Euston' to the east – both of which, astonishingly, operated as commercial rivals for over 40 years. Only in 1881 were the two sides directly linked to the main buildings: one J Maclaren designed a top-heavy classical pile surmounted by an odd-looking, pedimented clock tower which served to mask the original 1838 station entrance – keeping which feature clear of obstruction had been the main reason behind the two blocks.

By the mid-1840s hotels were often key constituents of the station site – as, for example, at Francis Thompson's Midland Hotel at Derby of 1841 (Fig 1.15). Though Thompson's station (Fig 1.16) has been demolished, in one

of the most shameful sagas in British railway history, its Grade II-listed hotel, with its handsome, seven-bay brick frontage and a porch of Doric pilasters, is still in its original use today as Britain's oldest surviving station hotel. Other station hotels were later crammed into the pre-existing site; thus the large 'mansion' at the centre of J P Pritchett's splendid Hull Paragon of 1849 was subsequently retro-fitted as a hotel.

The station hotel was not, in its early years, always owned by the railway. Nor was the hotel always incorporated into the station footprint – as, for example, was the case with Lewis Cubitt's stand-alone Great Northern Hotel at King's Cross of 1854 (Fig 1.17). However, by 1860 hotels usually formed an integral part of the main station site, as at York, Charing Cross, Cannon Street and, most famously, St Pancras. In 1953 the architectural critic H S Goodhart-Rendel dismissed E M Barry's hotel fronting Charing Cross Station (Fig 1.18) as a stripy pile of sandwiches.

Fig 1.18
E M Barry's Charing Cross
Hotel, pictured in 1887.
(BL08166)

Nor did station hotels necessarily harmonise with the architectural idiom of the trainshed behind. Thus P C Hardwick's vaguely French Great Western Hotel at Paddington of 1854 (Fig 1.19) had little in common with Brunel, Wyatt and Jones's bravura composition behind it; J W Livock's four-square classical pile, the Queens Hotel at Birmingham New Street (Fig 1.20), never aspired to the soaring ambitions of Cowper's radical trainshed; while J T Knowles's Grosvenor Hotel at Victoria of 1860–1 (Fig 1.21) maximised the number of rooms available rather than making any attempt to lend a railway air to its looming 'Renaissance' elevations. On occasion the hotel could even eclipse the shed. Thus the soaring, Gothic hotel which J W Waterhouse built in

Fig 1.19
P C Hardwick's Great
Western Royal Hotel at
Paddington of 1854 looked
rather more effective seen
here in c 1880, before the
depredations of the 1930s
and the post-war era.
(CC97/01711)

Fig 1.20
The much-altered Queen's
Hotel, which fronted
Birmingham New Street
Station from 1854 until
1964.
(BB66/3259)

Fig 1.21
The cliff-like façade of
Knowles's Grosvenor Hotel
at Victoria of 1860–1.
(AA061780)

17

Fig 1.22
J W Waterhouse's ambitious
Great North Western Hotel
at Liverpool Lime Street,
opened in 1871.
(BB70/07024)

1871 to serve Liverpool Lime Street (Fig 1.22) is now more famous than the William Baker trainshed which lurks obliquely behind.

Boldness and enterprise

Philip Hardwick

When the early railways sought to convince potential passengers of the safety and stability of their enterprise, they invariably turned to experienced, classically trained architects. Thus, when the London and Birmingham Railway (L&BR) – the world's first long-distance, main-line route – sought to anchor its bold new scheme to buildings by a well-known, high-profile architect, they chose Philip Hardwick.

London-born Hardwick's architectural lineage was impeccable. He had been trained as an architect under his father, Thomas Hardwick, who had been a pupil of William Chambers, and whom James Wyatt affectionately termed 'a regular bred, classical architect'.[1] His grandfather, moreover, had been a master mason who had worked for all the great names of the second half of the 18th century, among them Robert and John Adam. After studying in

France and Italy, Philip Hardwick began in 1819 to inherit jobs from his father; he built a series of churches in both classical and Gothic styles, and was appointed surveyor to a number of London estates. In 1829, the year of his father's death, Hardwick won the commission for a new livery hall for the Goldsmith's Company in the City of London, which was completed in 1835. In 1831 he was elected a fellow of the Royal Society and, in 1834, he was a founding member of the Institute of British Architects. Hardwick's fine, neoclassical landmark of Goldsmith's Hall in the City of London had barely been completed when he was approached by the directors of the L&BR to be their in-house architect – the first such appointment in the country. In this capacity Hardwick was charged with designing the railway's first two termini at either end of the line.

Birmingham Curzon Street (Fig 2.1) was built in 1838 at the L&BR's northern boundary.

Fig 2.1
The proud entrance to Hardwick's Birmingham Curzon Street of 1838, still standing proudly long after the passengers have deserted it.
(BB64/02095)

Hardwick's Ionic portico was meant to complement his Doric entrance to Euston, and accordingly fronted the station buildings rather than being integral to them (thus enabling a more barbaric age to demolish the rest of the station). Much of its purpose, however, evaporated in 1854, when New Street Station was built half a mile to the west as the principal terminus for what was now the London and North Western Railway (LNWR). Passenger services ceased in 1893, but it survived as a goods station until 1966, after which all but Hardwick's porticoed pavilion was demolished. Today the triumphal arch stands marooned in a sea of urban desolation, hosting the odd art exhibition. Many schemes – including incorporating the structure into the adjacent Millennium Point campus of Birmingham City University – have been mooted for its rescue, but at the time of writing none has begun. One possible ray of hope lies in giving the building a starring role in the station complex designed to serve the High Speed 2 route, currently planned between London and Manchester.

At the southern end of the L&BR's line, Hardwick designed the most celebrated of all railway monuments. The severe, Doric, pedimented Euston Arch (Fig 2.2) was, it has often been pedantically pointed out, not strictly an arch but actually a 22m (72ft) propylaeum (an entrance gateway to a courtyard). Completed in May 1838, it cost £35,000 – prompting the functionalist developer-architect Thomas Cubitt (the brother of King's Cross's Lewis) to comment that 'a good station could be built at King's Cross for less than the cost of the ornamental archway at Euston Square'. In France, Auguste Perdonnet's *Traité élémentaire des chemins de fer* of 1855 snorted that 'an arch of triumph of that sort had no connection whatsoever with the purpose of a railway'. Francis Whishaw, though, perceptively declared that the arch 'is the key, as it were, to all the railways of London', while William Acworth's classic and indispensable *Railways of England* of 1889 rightly lauded the arch's 'national character'. And while the Gothic messiah, A W N Pugin, saw the Euston Arch merely as 'a piece of Brobdignagian absurdity which must have cost the company a sum which would have built a first-rate station, replete with convenience, and which would have been really grand from its simplicity', in 1839 critic John

Fig 2.2
Philip Hardwick's celebrated, and much-lamented, Euston Arch. (DD84/00001)

Britton recognised the quality and purpose of a monument which the L&BR directors had themselves praised as 'well adapted to the national character of the undertaking', hymning the arch as 'a most successful adaptation of the pure Grecian Doric; admirably suited, by its massiveness and boldness of its design and execution, for an approach … connecting the British Metropolis with the most important towns of the kingdom'.[2]

As Philip Hardwick had been greatly assisted in launching his architectural career by *his* father, so he ensured that his own son, Philip Charles, gradually took on more responsibility for his office's projects. Thus the magnificent Great Hall and Board Room at Euston Station, opened in 1849, were entrusted to Hardwick junior. Philip Charles's Great Hall (Fig 2.3) employed direct references to the antique

Fig 2.3
P C Hardwick's magnificent Great Hall at Euston, photographed in the 1930s. (10305173 © National Railway Museum/Science & Society Picture Library – All rights reserved)

world in the best neoclassical tradition to create an imposing interior that also functioned as a highly efficient welcoming and dispersal area. It was 42m (139ft) long and 18.9m (62ft) wide, and lined with a 6m (20ft)-high colonnade of Ionic columns painted to resemble red granite shafts, with white marble capitals, the scale of the hall's interior recalled the basilicas and baths of Ancient Rome, while its double-cube proportions mirrored those of Inigo Jones's Whitehall Banqueting House of 1622–9. The Hall's plaster ceiling, whose design was taken directly from the fourth-century basilica of St Paul's outside the walls in Rome had, in 1849, the largest span of any ceiling in the world. Some of its 'Roman' ceiling panels were even perforated to allow the hot water pipes behind to help heat and ventilate the hall. On the walls, the eight large plaster bas-reliefs depicting the principal destinations of the railway were designed by John Thomas, the Prince Consort's favourite sculptor, who was then working simultaneously for Buckingham Palace and the new Palace of Westminster. Thomas also designed the statue of George Stephenson which originally commanded the Great Hall.

Disappointingly, the rest of Euston Station grew somewhat haphazardly during the 1860s and 1870s. As the station's biographer, K J Ellaway, has noted: 'From its first simple departure and arrival platforms the station gradually groped its way to the east and west until it was contained within a rough rectangle'. Hardwick's marvellous hall did not line up with his father's arch, and the subsequent westward development of the station left what was supposed to be a central concourse 'something of a hidden treasure, tucked away in the cheap wrapping paper of subsequent decades'.[3]

Philip Hardwick was not the only nationally renowned figure to be enlisted by the new, ambitious railway companies to endow their audacious plans with a veneer of architectural pedigree. What was to become the London and South Western Railway (LSWR) selected the versatile William Tite, an experienced architect who could design adeptly in seemingly any style, and the city of Newcastle inevitably turned to the brilliant local practitioner, John Dobson. But, in 1835, the directors of the new London-to-Bristol railway scheme alighted on the brilliant but controversial – and astonishingly young – figure of Isambard Kingdom Brunel.

Isambard Kingdom Brunel

The son of the emigré French engineer, Marc Brunel, I K Brunel (1806–59) was educated in France, at the College of Caen and the mathematical hothouse of the Lycée Henri-Quatre in Paris, and was apprenticed to scientific instrument maker, Louis Breguet, before rejoining his father in England in 1799 (where his father had emigrated after a six-year stay in America). In 1827, aged only 21, his father put Isambard in charge of a mass of labourers as resident engineer at the Thames Tunnel. In January 1828, a flood of the workings killed six men and seriously injured Isambard himself, who came to Bristol to recuperate. Living in the select Bristol suburb of Clifton – where he also conceived the idea of a suspension bridge across the Avon Gorge, a sum for which had been bequeathed by the merchant William Vick decades earlier – Brunel's familiarity with the city and its leading citizens helped him make the right connections. Consequently, in 1833, aged 27, he was appointed engineer for the nascent Great Western Railway (GWR) then being proposed between Bristol and the capital. Brunel subsequently surveyed every mile of the route of the railway himself, both before and after government assent for the project was won in 1835. However, his decision to select a direct route which passed through no major towns east of Bath and west of Reading, but which offered a flatter track with fewer major engineering obstacles, as well as potential branch connections to Oxford, Newbury and Gloucester – let alone his decision to plump for a far broader track gauge than that of his rivals – was to cause decades of controversy.

Brunel's personal achievement was astonishing. His railway had the fewest inclines of any major route, so as to make long-term savings on coal consumption, and featured prodigious engineering triumphs such as the Wharncliffe Viaduct in Hanwell of 1836–7, Maidenhead Bridge of 1838–9 (which included two of the largest and flattest brick arches yet built) and the Box Tunnel of 1841. It also, however, incorporated a fatal flaw – one which would ensure that the railway would descend into perennial unprofitability by the end of the century. Where other railway companies had agreed building tracks on the so-called 'standard' gauge of 4ft 8½in (1.4m), Brunel stubbornly selected a broad gauge of 7ft ¼in (2.1m) – a solution which would, he asserted, ensure a more steady and comfortable ride. By the time of Brunel's death in 1859 – aged only 53, and worn out by work – it was clear that the GWR had lost the 'gauge war'. The GWR's subsequent conversion to standard gauge (which was only completed in 1892) crippled the railway's finances during the latter decades of the 19th century.

Brunel's insistence on sticking to a broad gauge that would serve his passengers' – if not his shareholders' – best interests says much about his difficult management style. He was a notoriously hard taskmaster to others, and was particularly poor at delegating. While it seems incredible that the design of the whole of the GWR's physical infrastructure – lines, embankments, tunnels, bridges and sheds, as well as stations – was all designed by Brunel himself, this astonishing claim is largely true. Brunel did work with collaborating architects and engineers; at Paddington, for example, T A Bertram undertook much of the day-to-day project work, whilst Matthew Digby Wyatt was hired to realise much of the station's ornamentation. However, Brunel was generally what we would call today an inveterate micro-manager. As architectural historian Steven Brindle has noted, Brunel was involved at every stage of the work, and was notoriously unable to delegate detail: he negotiated with landowners, wrote (and proofread) the contracts and supervised the contractors. Brindle concludes that 'The obverse of Brunel's Olympian self-confidence and decisiveness was an unwillingness to recognize others as equals.'[4] Famously, this even included Brunel's great railway rival: Robert Stephenson of the London and Birmingham.

Brunel believed he could do it all – and indeed he did. The celebrated bridge builder, shipbuilder and railway engineer also tried his hand, very successfully, at architecture. Not only did he have a role in many of the smaller town and country stations along the route: when the first GWR train steamed into its Bristol destination on 30 June 1841 (typically, before the station was actually finished), it was into a Brunel-designed terminus. Temple Meads Station of 1839–41 was provided with an impressive, stone Tudor street elevation and a wooden Tudor/Gothic trainshed. The latter, with its span of 22m (72ft), its Tudor colonnade and its fake hammerbeams and pendants straight from Westminster Hall and Hampton Court, was allegedly inspired by the city's fine Gothic architecture – notably the nearby Gothic masterpiece of St Mary Redcliffe – and certainly

made an appropriate addition to the city's fine building tradition. At Temple Meads, Brunel's aim was to separate arriving and departing passengers – much as America's great Beaux Arts railway termini sought to achieve 70 years later. Thus, as has been noted, one side of the station was reserved for arrivals, and one for departures, with the three-storey head-building on Temple Gate accommodating the necessary services and the railway offices. Brunel also wanted the design to reflect the status and ambitions of the GWR, and proposed a number of variants of Tudor Gothic. His suggestion of large, castellated pavilion-towers as bookends at either end of the station's principal façade, however, alarmed the cost-minded GWR directors, and his scheme was watered down to just two Tudor gateways to the north and south of the elevation.

A W N Pugin, predictably, was appalled at Brunel's harnessing of late medieval forms for the service of a mere railway. He called the result a 'mere caricature', and 'a design at once costly and offensive and full of pretension'. Modern commentators have been more generous, however. David Lloyd and Donald Insall declaring Brunel's Temple Meads to be 'without parallel in early railway architecture'.

In 1852, Brunel's ground-breaking station was provided with a rival just two hundred yards to the south: the new terminus of the Bristol and Exeter Railway (B&ER) (Fig 2.4). The B&ER's trains had initially used Brunel's GWR station. But now, with the increase in traffic (in 1854 the Midland Railway had arrived at Temple Meads, too), the B&ER decided that the company needed its own, discrete terminus. Brunel had surveyed the B&ER's proposed route and, until 1849, the B&ER's line had been worked by GWR stock. But the new station was not built to Brunel's design. Like Brunel's terminus, the B&ER station was built of local stone, and looked to Bristol's architectural past for its inspiration. But that was where the similarity ended. In contrast to Brunel's long, low elevation, local architect Samuel Fripp (surely a name straight out of Dickens?) created an ambitious, soaring essay in domestic Jacobean, with two tall, jaunty turrets flanking an entrance which featured both a Dutch gable and paired Doric columns.

By the mid-1860s growth in traffic meant that Brunel's station could not cope and plans were made for a new station, which would combine the GWR and B&ER lines, to be built

Fig 2.4 (above)
Bristol Temple Meads
photographed by Reece
Winstone in the 1890s.
Brunel's original terminus is
on the left, Fripp's building
for the Bristol and Exeter
Railway is on the right, and
Wyatt's new unified station
is at the centre.
(OB1283 © Reece Winstone
Archive)

Fig 2.5 (opposite top)
A rare survival of a Brunel
'chalet' station: Culham in
Oxfordshire, of 1844.
(BB92/01174)

Fig 2.6 (opposite bottom)
Bradford-on-Avon Station in
Somerset in its heyday.
(RO/07707/001)

to the east of both termini – and for which Brunel's original station would become a mere and much-diminished north-western adjunct. The executing engineer for this extension, completed in 1878 (by which time the GWR had absorbed the B&ER, thus obviating the need for a separate B&ER terminus to the south), was the GWR's Francis Fox – who may thus have been the designer of the splendid, curved, iron trainshed. The design of the new entrance building, phrased in a Brunel-esque Tudor Gothic but provided with a pinnacled clock tower topped with a pyramidal French roof, has been attributed to Matthew Digby Wyatt – formerly Brunel's assistant – though there is no documentary evidence to support this. Between 1932 and 1935, Fox's station was extended south and east by the GWR's in-house architect, P A Culverhouse. (Culverhouse simultaneously expanded Paddington and was the architect of the imposing art deco station at Leamington Spa.) And, soon after 1945, Wyatt's Noddy-like pyramidal roof atop his entrance tower, which had been seriously damaged by enemy bombing in 1940, was dismantled. Twenty years later, Brunel's station was closed, and a modern signal box crassly built across the entrance to his original ter-

minus. Brunel's building, depressingly, served as a car park for years, although in 1981 the building was rescued from demolition by the Brunel Engineering Centre Trust, who took on a 99-year lease from British Rail but who failed to find a viable use: the science activity area known as 'The Exploratory' was closed in 1999 after a decade of operation, while the British Empire and Commonwealth Museum opened in 2002, but folded in 2008. At the time of writing plans are finally being prepared to restore the trainshed as part of the working station for the first time since the 1960s.

Whilst Brunel's Temple Meads still endures, many of Brunel's smaller GWR stations do not. This is partly because Brunel's station houses were generally detached from the main station building; thus, when his GWR stations were closed in the post-war years, they proved too small to convert for residential use. Thus was Brunel's architectural economy ultimately hoisted by its own petard. However, Culham in Oxfordshire, of 1844 (Fig 2.5), and Bradford-on-Avon in Somerset, of 1858 (Fig 2.6), still survive as examples of Brunel's 'chalet' station idiom: small, asymmetrical Tudor or Italianate buildings executed in red brick or stone with grey slate roofs, triangular gables

Fig 2.7
Southam Road and Harbury
in Warwickshire, a Brunel
country station demolished
50 years ago.
(RO/06249/001)

Fig 2.8
Brunel's station of 1848 at
Mortimer in Berkshire –
now happily still extant.
(BB98/11893)

and broad, overhanging awnings. Many GWR 'chalet' stations – for example, at Brimscombe in Gloucestershire, Minety and Ashton Keynes in Wiltshire and Southam Road and Harbury in Warwickshire (Fig 2.7) – have now been lost. However, a few of Brunel's slightly larger 'roadside' stations, characterised by their low, hipped roofs, are still with us – a roster which includes Mortimer in Berkshire, of 1848 (Fig 2.8), Torre in Devon, of 1857, and Charlbury in Oxfordshire, of 1853 (Fig 2.9), the last remaining wooden 'roadside' building.

Brunel's GWR provided some of its medium-sized stations with overall wooden trainsheds. Today, just one remains: at Frome in Somerset (Fig 2.10). Built in *c* 1850, its roof's wooden rafters are today held in place by iron tie rods. The concept was Brunel's, but in this case the executant architect was J R Hannaford. The wooden overall roof – now of corrugated iron – covered both tracks, and is a reminder of a time when railways thought more of the comfort of their passengers than of the need to cut costs and thereby maximise shareholders' dividends

Fig 2.9
The important wooden station at Charlbury, Oxon, of 1853.
(RO/07298/001)

Fig 2.10
Frome in Somerset, of c *1850: the last GWR station which retains its overall wooden roof today.*
(RO/02800/002)

and directors' salaries. At Chard Central, Brunel designed a low, handsome symmetrical Italianate station whose round arches of the main elevation are reflected in the supports for the overall roof behind. He used the same format, albeit in a more haphazard and asymmetrical way, at Taplow and Marlow. Chard Central survives as offices, although the line has long gone, and Taplow is still with us; but although the Marlow branch still operates, trains run to and from a tarmacked platform, the fine Brunel station having been demolished soon after 1967.

Brunel had, predictably, ensured that he was the principal designer of the GWR's London terminus. Here, he used the contractors whom Sir Joseph Paxton had used at his Crystal Palace of 1851: Fox, Henderson & Co. Brunel had been a member of the Great Exhibition building committee, so was very familiar both with the contractors and with Paxton's revolutionary iron-and-glass building. As Steven Brindle has noted, 'In effect, Brunel engaged the team who were building the Crystal Palace to build Paddington'.[5] The obvious exception was Paxton himself: the Crystal Palace's architect was a director of the Midland Railway, and thus could not work for a rival concern. It is also doubtful if Brunel could have endured the presence of a similarly experienced and opinionated character on his pet project.

Fig 2.11
London Paddington: Brunel, Wyatt and Jones's splendid trainshed roof in 1965. (AA062048)

The resulting trainshed at Paddington (Fig 2.11) was, David Lloyd considered, one of the wonders of British architecture. It was the first real cathedral of the Railway Age: it even had transepts. The columns supporting the innovatory, ridge-and-furrow glazed roof carried hidden rainwater downpipes, which drained underneath the concourse floor. The roof's iron beams were themselves pierced with geometric shapes – not just for decoration, but to assist the cleaners fit the scaffolding necessary to clean this highly complex structure.

But Paddington was not wholly Brunel's work. Much of the iron detailing on the spandrels of the vaulting and on the trainshed's windscreen – where the shapes were more Moorish than Gothic – appears to have been designed by M D Wyatt. Christian Barman wrote of Wyatt's reworked shed that:

it is a unique work of art, remarkable for many qualities but above all for a unity of architectural treatment that is not to be found in any other iron station. His detail flows freely and fluently from the ridge of the great elliptical arches with their six graceful crossings down the long lattice girders to the octagonal pillars of the well-spaced colonnades.[6]

Wyatt in turn hired Owen Jones (yet another designer who had worked on the Crystal Palace) to advise on colouring the ironwork in a striking yet medievally inspired palette. Wyatt's involvement did not, however, mean that Brunel was delegating all of the station's decoration to another hand. Recent examination of the detailed drawings for Paddington suggests that in many cases – such as the design of the innovative oriel windows on the western departure platform (now Platform 1), with their distinctive, round-headed lights – Wyatt was simply working up the sketches already made by Brunel. The vaguely Arabic shape of much of the ironwork does, at least, seem to have been solely Wyatt's invention.

Brunel's achievement was blessed by royal patronage. Queen Victoria arrived here on her first railway journey (from Slough) on 13 June 1842, and frequently used the line – in preference to the more tortuous journey via the LSWR route from Windsor – after 1854. The royal waiting room on the departure platform at Paddington now houses the First Class Lounge. It was from this platform that Victoria made her last journey, on 2 February 1901, in her splendid funeral train.

Disappointingly, the station hotel that the GWR added to the south of Brunel's concourse at Paddington not only had little in common with Brunel and Wyatt's railway-accented idiom, but also made an equivocal impression on Praed Street. The façade of P C Hardwick's Great Western Royal Hotel (see Fig 1.19), with its distinctly undersized pediment, lacked a powerful, central emphasis. The blame for some of this can be laid at the feet of the GWR's P A Culverhouse, who removed some of Hardwick's decoration and refaced the whole façade in his favoured Patent Victoria pre-cast stone, a mix of cement and ground granite, between 1930 and 1935. Hardwick's interiors had been magnificent when the hotel opened in 1854. It was then one of the capital's most luxurious staging posts, being equipped with such unheard-of luxuries as electric clocks and bells, and fireproof staircases. In the 1930s, however, Culverhouse destroyed most of these original interiors, including the splendid, two-storey coffee room, and substituted a number of low-ceilinged spaces phrased in a modish, diluted art deco manner.

Sir William Tite

The third well-established architect to turn his hand to station design in the 1830s and 1840s was Sir William Tite (1798–1873). The son of a Russian merchant and the pupil of the workmanlike Scottish mason-turned-architect David Laing, Tite was admitted to the Royal Academy Schools in 1818 and launched his own practice with his design for Mill Hill School of 1825. However, while he made his name internationally with the Royal Exchange in London of 1842–4, it was Tite's railway work that provided the bulk of his practice's income. A keen architectural politician and parliamentary figure – he was MP for Bath between 1855 and 1870 – Tite was elected President of the Architectural Society in 1838, made President of the Royal Institute of British Architects from 1861 to 1863 (and again between 1867 and 1870), and knighted in 1869. In 1860 he led a high-powered delegation to the Prime Minister, designed to lobby Lord Palmerston to oppose George Gilbert Scott's Gothic design for the new Foreign Office. In this he was successful; but his reaction to Scott's subsequent Gothic spectacle at St Pancras, begun a year before he received his knighthood, is sadly unrecorded.

Fig 2.12
William Tite's first station at Southampton, of 1839. (RO/08058/003)

Tite's first major railway commission was for the London and Southampton Railway, which in 1839 metamorphosed into the LSWR. His Southampton Station (Fig 2.12) opened in June 1839 (although services did not begin until the track was completed in May 1840). Now one of the earliest surviving railway buildings in England, the station was designed in the form of an Italian town palace. Its five-bay, three-storey façade was assertive yet familiar – its projecting, rusticated porte cochère of five arches recalled both Vicenza's townhouses and the arcades of Inigo Jones's Covent Garden. Closed in 1966, only the façade remains; its interior now serves as a casino.

Fig 2.13 (above)
Tite's domestically phrased station at Micheldever, Hampshire, shown in penurious Southern days in 1926. (BL28886/008)

Fig 2.14 (right)
Chiswick of 1849, with Tite's classical station building on the left. (RO/22130/001)

Most of Tite's subsequent railway work was also executed for the LSWR. Many of his early LSWR stations, such as Micheldever (Fig 2.13) and Winchester, both of 1840, and Chiswick, of 1849 (Fig 2.14), were conceived as handsome, solid, classical villas, with awnings attached on both sides for external arrivals and as platform cover. This format was also applied after 1847 to the LSWR stations on the new route between Basingstoke and Salisbury. Larger LSWR stations, such as Netley and Chertsey, were built as seven-bay compositions in the domestic manner, with two projecting wings, each of two bays, and a prominent awning over the entrance. This standard configuration was subsequently not only reproduced elsewhere on the LSWR, but also borrowed by the neighbouring London, Brighton and South Coast Railway (LBSCR) for many of their Sussex coastal stations.

Occasionally, Tite escaped from standardisation. His Dorchester South of 1847 (Fig 2.15) was more ambitious than anything since Southampton: a long, single-storey structure with plaster pilasters across the entrance elevation. At Gosport of 1841, Tite daringly introduced a 14-bay Tuscan colonnade, stretching from a rusticated entrance pavilion adapted from Southampton's porte cochère. Exactly a century later, however, on the night of 10 March 1941, the station received a direct hit from a German incendiary bomb, which destroyed the roof. British Railways made little attempt to rescue this fine building (Fig 2.16) and, on 6 June 1953, scheduled passenger services from Gosport ceased (freight traffic continuing until

Fig 2.15 (above)
Tite's Dorchester South in
c 1930.
(RO/06762/001)

Fig 2.16 (below)
The forlorn remains of Tite's
grand Tuscan colonnade
at Gosport, shown in the
1960s.
(RO/02467/001)

Fig 2.17 (below top)
Tudor Gothic at the LSWR's
Crewkerne Station.
(RO/07994/002)

Fig 2.18 (below bottom)
Whimple Station before its
mutilation.
(RO/08142/001)

1969). After years of increasing dereliction, planning approval was given in 2006 for the Guinness Trust to convert the platforms and buildings into a small number of residential properties and offices, which was executed by architect Matt Swanton of award-winning architects Format Milton Architects (subsequently rebadged as Re-Format).

Tite did not just limit himself to Italianate classicism. His Barnes Station of 1846 was a soaring, asymmetrical Tudor brick building with grid windows, a four-centred doorway and diaper brickwork, whose verticality was accentuated by its dominant chimney stacks and tall gables. It was one of four picturesque Tudor Gothic brick stations built by Tite for this route – the others were Putney, Mortlake and Richmond – but today is the only survivor. And, while Barnes is still busy, the original Tite building survives only in private hands.

Fig 2.19
Tite's tongue-in-cheek
Tudorist pastiche at Windsor
and Eton Riverside.
(Taken from David A
Ingham collection, original
photographer unknown)

Tite also used Tudor Gothic for much of the Yeovil and Exeter line of the LSWR. Some of these stations – such as Crewkerne of 1860 (Fig 2.17), with its tall, three-storey gabled tower, and Axminster, also of 1860, with its Tudor grid windows, asymmetrical brick gables (now mercifully free of their 1960s paint finish) and stone surrounds – survive in something like their original form; others, such as Whimple (Fig 2.18), are barely recognisable.

Perhaps Tite's most playful Gothic station was at Windsor and Eton Riverside (Fig 2.19): an engaging, Tudorist composition of 1849. Passengers arrived under a grand, Tudor-arched porte cochère, whilst a vast Tudor window lit the booking hall. As the long, buttressed, station wall stretched northwards, its brickwork featured diaper patterns which spelt out the monograms of the current monarch and her consort. The diaper work also included the initials 'WC' – not for the nearby castle but for the railway's chairman, William Chaplin, along with 'LSWR', and 'WT' for Tite himself. At the end of this north wall perched a jaunty stone-capped turret, built to give LSWR staff a good vantage point from where they could spot the Queen's carriage emerging from Windsor Castle. Beneath this turret was, appropriately enough, the royal waiting room.

Tite used the same grand, rectangular Tudor windows he had used at Windsor and Eton Riverside for the two flanking, gable-end pavilions which made the entrance front to his Penrith of 1848 – for the Lancaster and Carlisle railway – so imposing. Tite's Tudorist masterpiece, though, was his Carlisle Citadel of 1847–8. Built in fine, local red sandstone, its grand, five-bay, buttressed porte cochère (an exuberantly Gothic version of his rusticated arcade at Southampton) was nicely complemented by a fine, ecclesiastical-looking clock tower topped by an open stone octagon.

Other railway architects

John Dobson

Across the Pennines, local architect John Dobson – in Christian Barman's view 'the greatest of all railway architects'[7] – was simultaneously creating a classical tour-de-force at Newcastle. Dobson (1787–1865), born in North Shields, could have been a national player. Venturing to London in 1809, he studied under the watercolourist John Varley; but while his friend, Robert Smirke, urged him to stay in the capital, Dobson decided to return to the North-East, where he built an impressive number of churches, country houses and city terraces. Dobson's Newcastle Central Station of 1845–50, built in a commanding Doric style with a street façade

Fig 2.20
John Dobson's trainshed at
Newcastle Central.
(DP034473)

Fig 2.21
Thomas Prosser's imposing
portico at Newcastle: not
what Dobson had planned,
but still a fine monument.
(DP034472)

183m (600ft) long, was intended to be the central keystone of a vast, new, classical redevelopment of Newcastle city centre financed by the speculative builder Richard Grainger. Dobson's original scheme for the station offices included a huge portico in a more demonstrative Ionic style and a tall tower, neither of which was actually built. However, with the help of engineer Robert Stephenson, he was able to design not just the station's architectural frontage but also the enormous trainshed behind (Fig 2.20). The latter comprised three arched glass roofs, and was built in a curve on a 240m (800ft) radius. The end result was the first, true iron-and-glass vault on a giant scale – a structure in which, in Christian Barman's opinion, 'the English railway station reaches its highest moment of functional adventure and

discovery'.[8] Newcastle Central was the ancestor of all other great city station trainsheds: a stand-alone structure that did not rely on columns rising from the platforms (which could get in the way of the passengers), but which soared above both trains and passengers. And it was all Dobson's work; surpassing Cubitt's achievement at King's Cross, he designed not only the station's remarkable, neoclassical façade but, working closely with the ironwork contractors he had got to know well, created the magnificent, curving trainshed, too. As architectural historian Simon Bradley has observed, this was an extraordinary leap for a man born in 1787, whose first buildings were completed two decades before railway stations even existed.

Dobson's trainshed at Newcastle boasted the first station roof to use round-arched, rolled-iron ribs – a form of construction hitherto reserved for garden glasshouses such as Paxton's 'Great Stove' at Chatsworth of 1836–40 or Burton and Turner's Palm House at Kew of 1844–8. Its cast-iron columns, adorned with simple leaf capitals, supported low-curved segmental girders. For devising rollers to shape these girders, Dobson was even awarded a medal at the Paris Exhibition of 1855.

Thomas Prosser

After Dobson's death, in 1865, the North Eastern Railway (NER) – having, significantly, moved its offices from Newcastle to York – demanded that the size and cost of Dobson's station be scaled down. As a result, architect Thomas Prosser completed a smaller, though still well-proportioned porch in monumental Doric (Fig 2.21). Gordon Biddle and O S Nock, in their invaluable *The Railway Heritage of Britain*, claimed that, had Dobson's original scheme been executed, it would have resulted in one of the finest 19th-century classical buildings in Europe.

Having appropriated well-known, reputable architects in order to lend architectural lustre and respectability to their early stations, by the 1850s the railway companies, now more confident and securely established, began to appoint lesser-known figures to provide them with cheaper, in-house expertise. And the first railway to appoint an architect to a permanent internal position was the NER who, in 1854, appointed Thomas Prosser as their company architect. Prosser had trained in Ignatius Bonomi's Durham office, and had been

Dobson's clerk of works at Newcastle Central – which was where he came to the attention of the NER. For the railway he built Durham Station in 1857 (Fig 2.22): a tidy essay in Tudor Gothic with a battlemented, three-bay Gothic porte cochère. The impressive brick station at Hornsea Town of 1864 – dominated by its five-bay, pedimented porte cochère – may also be by Prosser, although the name of Rawlins Gould has also been suggested. Hornsea's platform awning disappeared soon after the station closed in 1964, but the rest of the main station building survives as offices (thanks to a restoration of the late 1980s), as does the three-bay station house, originally placed at right angles to the northernmost five-bay wing.

Prosser's best work was undoubtedly at York. Work on the new station began in 1872, although the ailing Prosser had to retire from the project due to ill-health in 1874 and the building was completed in 1877 by NER house architects Benjamin Burley and William Peachey, the latter also largely responsible for the imposing but dull station hotel next door. Prosser's head-building at York was dull and monotonous: the principal, street elevation was long and low, and the segmental arches of its glazed-roof porch were too flat for such a long frontage. It was, instead, the curved trainshed (Fig 2.23) that attracted plaudits, both then and now. The soaring iron-and-glass roof was supported on composite iron columns, whose decorated bracket spandrels carried the city arms and the white rose of Yorkshire.

Even Carroll Meeks found Prosser's trainshed 'unusually handsome'.[9] Some delightful minor features happily survive today, too, such as the windscreen of tiered arcaded lights at the end of the eastern aisle, between the tea rooms and the station hotel; the ceramic-tiled map of the NER network, set in a moulded tile frame; and the two large station clocks – that on the concourse side in a pedimented timber surround, that on the footbridge incorporating foliage, white roses and the City of York arms.

Fig 2.22
Prosser's Durham Station of 1857.
(AA56/04642)

Fig 2.23
The astonishing trainshed at York, shown in a highly atmospheric shot of c 1890.
(OP25562)

William Bell

Peachey's successor as chief architect at the NER in 1877 was William Bell (1844–1919). Peachey had lasted only six months at the NER: despite his strong Baptist background, he was dismissed for inflating costs for a new goods station at Stockton. Bell, however, spent his whole architectural career with the same company. He rebuilt Darlington Bank Top (today the town's sole main-line station) and Stockton Station in 1887 and 1893 respectively, Darlington's five-bay projecting porch being surmounted by a lofty, vaguely Wrennian clock tower (Fig 2.24). Bell added other, bizarre, Rhenish-looking clock towers at Manors in 1909 (a station scandalously demolished in 1978) and Whitley Bay of 1910 (thankfully still with us: the station is now part of the Tyne and Wear Metro system). And Bell's splendid 'greenhouse' trainshed at Tynemouth of 1882 (Fig 2.25), at risk for years (even though listed Grade II*), now hosts a weekly farmers' market. Tynemouth's arched canopies extend for about 200 yards, with a finely decorated roof apex and ornamental spandrels supported on eccentric iron columns with foliated capitals.

Perhaps William Bell's most admired work, though, was the new, partly tiled concourse at Hull Paragon of 1903–5. The original station had been designed by the NER's G T Andrews. Now, Bell designed a new trainshed and booking hall (complete with a freestanding wooden café with a wavy, coped parapet) in a delightful art nouveau idiom.

David Mocatta

While many of Bell's excellent station work survives, precious few of David Mocatta's buildings for the LBSCR survive today. Mocatta (1806–82), who came from a prominent Anglo-Jewish family and had been a pupil of John Soane in the 1820s, made the Italianate manner popular in Sussex during the 1840s. His most famous work was Brighton Station, the LBSCR's headquarters, but he also excelled in the small country stations he built for the new LBSCR lines. Even at Brighton, only a small part of his single-storey station remains; the trainshed (Fig 2.26) was rebuilt on a far larger scale by H E Wallis between 1882 and 1883, and Mocatta's main elevation (which soon became a rather incoherent façade) was swiftly obscured by a seven-bay iron canopy.

Fig 2.24
William Bell's Darlington Bank Top, completed in 1887.
(AA027050)

Fig 2.25
William Bell's joyous
trainshed at Tynemouth.
(RO/04377/006)

Fig 2.26
Brighton's 1880s trainshed,
pictured in c 1970.
(AA062904)

Francis Thompson

Francis Thompson, a native of Derby, initially worked for the North Midland Railway (NMR) in the 1840s (although he later built stations for a variety of companies), and built not only the first station at Derby of 1839–40 – the 'Tripartite Station' built not just for Hudson's NMR but also the Midland Counties and Birmingham and Derby Junction companies – but also the smaller stations on the NMR's route to Sheffield.

Thompson's early station buildings demonstrated his allegiance to the classical tradition of Robert Smirke and Philip Hardwick: they were simple, four-square block built as three- or four-bay houses with attached platform awnings. Some, such as Ambergate of 1840 (Fig 2.27) – a marvellous composition which was senselessly demolished in 1970 – were phrased in a more light-hearted Tudorbethan in the style of William Tite, though in Ambergate's case Thompson's astonishing, soaring Wrennian porch was never built. Others, like the now-derelict Wingfield (Fig 2.28), closed in 1967, were sober Greek pavilions. The architectural writer J C Loudon was most impressed

by Thompson's stations, hymning them as 'architectural gems' and 'standard models of cultivated design' in later editions of his hugely influential do-it-all guide, *An Encyclopaedia of Cottage, Farm and Villa Architecture* (originally published in 1833) and adapting Thompson's designs for stations like Ambergate and Wingfield into proposals for domestic villas.

Now the wheel had come full circle: railway architecture was influencing the design of the house, and not vice versa. In 1840, Whishaw admired Thompson's emerging stations, too, praising the NMR for ornamenting the line 'with so many beautiful villas, one of which would grace the sloping lawn of some domain by nature highly favoured' and lauding Derby – with its 'admirably contrived and elegant roofs' and 'spacious platforms' – as 'the most complete structure of the kind in the United Kingdom or, perhaps, in the world'.[10] A century later, Carroll Meeks was equally appreciative, albeit less euphoric, about Thompson's work:

The central motive is a pavilion with an arched recess framing the main entrance … Once established, the motive is repeated at intervals and in diminishing sizes, sometimes with doors, sometimes with

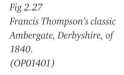

Fig 2.27
Francis Thompson's classic Ambergate, Derbyshire, of 1840.
(OP01401)

niches. The round-headed motive was repeated along the sides of the trainshed. In spite of the unity and simplicity of the scheme, however, nothing could mitigate the fact that though the façade was 1,050 feet long, it was only forty feet high.[11]

Whatever Professor Meeks's misgivings, at Derby Station Francis Thompson created the world's first complete railway complex, designing not just the station head-building and the tripartite trainshed behind but also adjacent workers' housing, a locomotive roundhouse, a railway workshop and a handsome hotel. Some of the housing survives, as does the Midland Hotel (now the 'Landmark'), a handsome, seven-bay brick composition with projecting end pavilions and a Doric porte cochère. But there is virtually no trace of Thompson's groundbreaking station at Derby today.

Thompson later went on to work with Robert Stephenson (who had been instrumental in getting Thompson his first job at the NMR), whom he assisted on projects such as the Britannia Bridge over the Menai Strait and the Chester and Holyhead Railway (CHR), of which Stephenson was principal engineer. Thompson designed Chester Station as a joint station for the CHR and two other local companies between 1847 and 1848, affording it a very long (13-bay), two-storey façade, which terminated in projecting pavilions topped with Italianate turrets with overhanging eaves. Thompson's later large stations, such as Ely of 1847 and Mostyn, Flintshire, of 1848 (closed in 1964 and long derelict, but now restored as a private home), were built to the same basic template: a long, low central building sandwiched between two taller pavilions. On his remarriage in 1853, Thompson emigrated to Canada, where he was appointed architect to the Grand Trunk Railway of Canada and the St Lawrence and Atlantic Railroad. He also built a railway terminus at Portland, Maine which, when it was opened in 1855, claimed to be the largest station in America.

Fig 2.28
Wingfield in Derbyshire: currently derelict but still standing.
(X79236)

Sancton Wood

Cambridge Station (Fig 2.29), built for the Eastern Counties Railway (ECR) in 1845, was long attributed to Francis Thompson. Now, evidence suggests that the designer was, instead, the enigmatic Great Eastern Railway (GER) house architect Sancton Wood (1815–86). As we have seen, until 2011 Cambridge was still worked as a single-sided station, with through trains arriving from both directions into a very long platform – today 470m (1,542ft) long. Equally boldly, the station building was fronted by a giant, 15-bay arcade of local white brick – an arcade

originally built as a porte cochère, but which is now enclosed.

Sancton Wood could turn his hand to Imperial Classicism – as seen at Dublin's Heuston Station of 1846 – or to a bizarre, castellated medievalism, as seen at his Inchicore Rail Works, also in Ireland and also of 1846. It is also likely that the eclectic Wood was the architect of the astonishingly powerful original Newmarket Station of 1848 (Fig 2.30), which had an imposing façade comprising a colonnade of eight sets of paired Ionic columns topped with massive entablature plinths and finials. The station was effectively replaced by a more centrally located alternative in 1879, after which

Fig 2.29
Cambridge Station in
c 1950.
(OP25563)

Fig 2.30
The magnificent colonnade
of paired columns at
Newmarket, of 1848. It is
inexcusable that this fine
building was demolished as
recently as 1980.
(RO/06002/001)

Fig 2.31
Sancton Wood's Bury St
Edmunds.
(RO/05840/6)

it hosted only race-day traffic until 1954 and goods traffic until 1967. But the station buildings survived until 1980 – when, despite their listed status, they were regrettably demolished. Today the site is a housing development.

Sancton Wood was also the architect – for the Eastern Union Railway – of the eccentric station at nearby Bury St Edmunds (Fig 2.31), of 1847, with its three pronounced arches over the entrance and its two unduly tall, neo-baroque towers flanking the tracks, and of the astonishing, asymmetrical Tudor assembly at Stamford Town (Fig 2.32), built for the Midland Railway between 1846 and 1848. This remarkable, neo-medieval composition, complete with tower and lantern at the east end and a tripartite arched entrance at the north, was judged by Biddle to be 'entirely worthy of the high standards of the town'. Fittingly, the booking hall now houses a railway bookshop.

Fig 2.32
Stamford Town: a fine
composition which now
also houses an invaluable
railway bookshop.
(DP044627)

Thomas Mainwaring Penson

While Sancton Wood's career remains tantalisingly enigmatic, we know rather more about T M Penson. Thomas Mainwaring Penson (1818–64) was born in Oswestry, Shropshire. The son of an architect-engineer with an extensive practice in North Wales, he subsequently took over his father's architectural office in Oswestry alongside his brother, Richard Kyrke Penson. Having been appointed as county surveyor of Cheshire, however, he moved to Chester, where he designed the Overleigh Cemetery, initiated the revival of black-and-

Fig 2.33
Thomas Penson's original design for Shrewsbury Station, before it was altered.
(BB99/06672)

Fig 2.34
Benjamin Green's Tweedmouth of 1847, demolished with indecent haste after closure in 1964.
(OP01476)

white half-timbering, and designed the Queen's Hotel opposite Thompson's station. In 1848 he designed Shrewsbury Station (Fig 2.33) for the Shrewsbury and Chester Railway: long, low and Tudoresque, like Thompson's Chester (the lower ground floor, introduced later to enable tunnels to reach under the platforms, has made it look taller than Penson originally devised), it featured four bays provided with four or five windows and one lonely, asymmetrical, pinnacled tower over the main entrance.

Benjamin Green

By the end of the 1840s, Tudor had become increasingly popular for all but the largest termini. One of the style's most fervent practitioners in the North-East was Benjamin Green (c 1811–58), who had been a pupil of A C Pugin (father of A W N Pugin) and who, from the 1830s, began to work in the office of his architect father, John G Green. Benjamin built a series of stately Tudor stations for the Newcastle and Carlisle, and Newcastle and Berwick railways in a distinctly domestic style. Unfortunately, the only examples to survive in anything like their original state are Morpeth of 1847, with its assertive, 'Scottish Baronial' gables, and Belford, also of c 1847, which boasts a three-bay, stripped-Gothic porch and a forest of bold chimneystacks. Perhaps his best work, at Tweedmouth (Fig 2.34), again of 1847, was demolished soon after the line was closed in 1964. Tragically, the strain of the architect's job took its toll on Benjamin Green (just as it had

with the younger Pugin only six years earlier). He survived his father by only six years, dying in a mental home in County Durham in 1858.

George Townsend Andrews

One of the Greens' principal architectural rivals in the North-East, George Townsend Andrews (1804–55), preferred to stick with Italianate classicism, yet could be stylistically omnivorous when let off the leash. Although born in Exeter, by the end of the 1820s Andrews had settled in York, where he became a friend of the notorious 'Railway King', George Hudson. Thanks to Hudson's influence, in one prodigious decade of enormous activity, from 1839 to 1849, Andrews designed most of the buildings, including the stations, for the York and North Midland (the precursor of the NER) as well as numerous stations for the Great North of England (GNER), the Newcastle and Darlington Junction and the York, Newcastle and Berwick railways. However, following the downfall of George Hudson in 1849, Andrews's practice ended abruptly, and, tarred by his close friendship with the disgraced Railway King, he built no more stations.

Andrews's station buildings were generally characterised by widely overhanging eaves, handsome Georgian proportions and low-hipped roofs. His handsome, well-mannered classicism can still be seen at Beverley of 1846 (Fig 2.35), with its single-storey Georgian entrance and its happily surviving overall, iron-trussed, hipped roof; and at Scarborough of 1844, whose orthodox, Grecian street frontage

Fig 2.35
G T Andrews's Beverley, with its still-surviving overall roof.
(RO/02858/001)

Fig 2.36
The eccentric, top-heavy station at Scarborough.
(BB99/11743)

Fig 2.37
Andrews's assured porte cochère at Whitby Station, of c 1850.
(BB93/29365)

Fig 2.38
Castle Howard Station not long before closure in 1930. (RO/05119/001)

Fig 2.39
Richmond, Yorkshire: monastic Gothic for the railways. (OP01450)

of three pedimented pavilions (each two bays wide – a classical solecism), connected by a series of long, low, nine-bay blocks, was made to appear ludicrous with the imposition of a massively oversized baroque clock tower atop the central pavilion in 1892 (Fig 2.36). Inside, however, Scarborough still retains Andrews's original, two-aisled, wood-and-glass roof.

Even more graceful than Scarborough was Andrews's Whitby of *c* 1850 (Fig 2.37), which was dominated by a giant, arched, five-bay stone porte cochère. But Andrews did not just espouse orthodox neoclassicism. At his Castle Howard Station of 1846 (Fig 2.38) – built to serve the Castle Howard estate – he indulged in a tongue-in-cheek pastiche of Vanbrughian baroque, infused with asymmetrical Italianate. Closed as early as 1930, and sold by British Rail in 1964, Castle Howard Station now offers residential and self-catering holiday accommodation.

However, as if to show that he was definitely not wedded to classicism, Andrews's Richmond Station of 1846–7 (Fig 2.39) was conceived as a monastic complex in Perpendicular Gothic, with a buttressed, five-bay porte cochère modelled on cathedral cloisters. The resulting station was, Biddle averred, 'like no other'. But this did not prevent the line from being closed by British Rail in 1969. Thankfully, the local council rescued the station building, which is now listed Grade II* and, after a spell as a garden centre,

*Fig 2.40 (right)
Andrews's assured,
Italianate masterpiece of
Hull Paragon.
(DP072610)*

*Fig 2.41 (opposite top)
The overall roof at Andrews's
Filey Station in the 1950s.
(RO/05141/002)*

it reopened on 9 November 2007 as an arts centre – with two cinema screens, a restaurant and café-bar, an art gallery, a heritage centre, a number of rooms for public use, and spaces for a range of artisan food producers.

Andrews's finest hour came with his design for Hull Paragon of 1848 (Fig 2.40). Here he created an Italian palazzo that more resembled a gentleman's club than a railway station – which, astonishingly, has managed to survive the vicissitudes of the subsequent years. Andrews's five-bay porte cochère, with four sets of coupled Tuscan columns between its arches, was later filled in to create a projecting ground floor. The ghastly, slab-like block of British Rail offices erected immediately to the south-east in

1962 has now, thankfully, gone, but the station now finds itself girded by a continuous shelter built by Holder Mathias in 2007. More recently, Martin Jennings's fine statue of Philip Larkin was placed in the concourse, in 2010.

In his brief career, the versatile Andrews also showed himself to be an adept engineer. At his Filey (Fig 2.41) and Beverley stations, the double-bowstring iron girders at each end of the trainshed may look hugely contemporary (especially in their new colour scheme of red and black), but are actually original, and demonstrate what a talented engineer Andrews was – the deceptively delicate girders enabling the two thin platform walls to carry his ponderous iron-and-glass roof.

William Tress

Italianate stations were, by 1850, ubiquitous down south, too. Tite's pupil, William Tress, adapted his master's classical formality for engaging Italianate stations in his designs for the South Eastern Railway (SER) of 1851–3.

Rye (Fig 2.42) was particularly successful: a recessed, triple-arched porch between two slightly projecting bays, each emphasised by heavy plaster quoins (and expressed both on the entrance and platform sides of the station), led to a taller, top-lit booking hall. At Wadhurst (Fig 2.43), of 1852, Tress provided what could have

Fig 2.42 (below)
William Tress's handsome and innovative station at Rye, Sussex.
(RO/06229/006)

been a plain, brick, two-storey domestic design with an engaging, Palladian double-pediment front, an approach he used again down the line at Stonegate. His greatest triumph, though, was at Battle, of 1852 (Fig 2.44). Here Tress used a cheekily domestic Gothic design to evoke the former splendours of the famous abbey nearby. The stationmaster's accommodation behind the

Fig 2.43
Tress's Wadhurst, of 1852.
(RO/06241/002)

Fig 2.44
William Tress's marvellous medieval station at Battle.
(OP01405)

projecting north gable was lit by grouped Early English lancets, while the booking hall – which boasted a collar-braced roof – was illuminated by two large Decorated-style windows. At Battle, Tress found the ideal balance between the new technology of the Victorian era and the rich architectural tradition of England's past.

John William Livock

While the great classical statements at either end of the L&BR were commissioned from the established Georgian architect Philip Hardwick, for many of its station buildings L&BR turned to the little-known John William Livock. Stations such as Livock's Oundle, of 1845 (Fig 2.45) (now a private residence: passenger traffic ceased in 1964) were invariably couched in a flamboyant Jacobean style, with tall Dutch gables on both entrance and platform elevations. In 1845, at Wansford, in Cambridgeshire (Fig 2.46), Livock built (for a village of just 400 people) a grandiose, stone-walled Jacobean pile. The station closed in

Fig 2.45
Oundle, Northants, before closure.
(RO/02891/001)

Fig 2.46
J W Livock's ambitious station at Wansford, Cambridgeshire.
(RO/17299/003)

1957, and Livock's buildings were sold to a haulage company. However, the station is now the headquarters of the Nene Valley Railway that, in 1995, opened a new-build structure on the opposite platform, and which is trying to buy back Livock's masterpiece. (Wansford's waiting room of 1884 actually comes from Barnwell Station in Northamptonshire.)

Livock was perhaps best known in his lifetime for his work at New Street Station in Birmingham, where he was responsible for the massive Grand Central Hotel (later renamed the 'Queens and North Western', and later just the Queens). This was built not in a playful Jacobean idiom but in a deadly serious and rather bland Renaissance palazzo style. The hotel and the station – the trainshed, as we have seen, possessed the largest iron-and-glass roofspan in the world when it opened in 1854 – were both demolished between 1964 and 1966, the trainshed roof having been largely destroyed by German bombing in 1940. It made way for that most dispiriting of British stations – designed by Kenneth Davies, lead planner for the London Midland Region (LMR) at British Rail – the mean and gloomy New Street of 1967, itself crushed under the weight of Cotton, Ballard and Blow's dismal, downmarket Pallasades (sic) Shopping Centre.

Frederick Barnes

In complete contrast to Livock's New Street were the East Anglian stations of Frederick Barnes (1824–84), an Ipswich architect who had trained in London under Sydney Smirke. Most prominent of these was the jolly Jacobean of Stowmarket of 1849, with its prominent Dutch gables and octagonal turrets sited at either end of the principal façade. Elsewhere in Suffolk, Frederick Barnes built for the Ipswich and Bury Railway (later absorbed into the GER) substantial, two-towered Tudor piles at Thurston (1845) and Needham (1846) (Fig 2.47). The latter comprised a house for the stationmaster on one side and a house for the head porter on the other. Its two-storey gables, punctuated by large, projecting 'Tudor' bays, were dramatically flanked by castellated towers, whilst the arched entrance in the middle of the composition was given an imposing, rusticated stone surround and topped by a triangular gable. While the station buildings at Needham (now Needham Market) were made redundant in 1967, they were subsequently listed and, happily, survive in private hands – the most recent restoration winning one of 2002's National Railway Heritage Awards. A more instructive contrast with the fate of Birmingham New Street is hard to find.

Fig 2.47
Frederick Barnes's superb Needham Market Station of 1846, pictured in 1957. (AA98/10943)

3

The country station

In 1986, social historians Jeffrey Richards and John MacKenzie hymned the country station as 'a thing of beauty',[1] and an institution that was uniquely English. Almost 40 years before – and shortly before many of the historic stations it praised were to disappear for ever – Christian Barman had declared that it was only in the English country station that 'the special idiom of railway architecture is to be found in its strongest and purest form', and that 'no country in the world has a collection of minor stations that can begin to compare with ours for sheer quality'.[2]

The unique assortment of buildings that comprised the English railway station – each different, yet each with many typological similarities – had, of course, been drastically reduced in number by the time Richards and MacKenzie's volume was published. Indeed, it was the country station which inevitably bore the brunt of the network cuts of the 1960s: around 5,000 of 7,000 stations which existed in Britain prior to the Beeching Report were sited in rural areas. Some, admittedly, were little more than cottages for the stationmaster, with an extra room designated for railway business. Others comprised little more than a booking office, a small waiting room and an office for the ticket clerk – who might be the only official to deal with all the aspects of passenger operation. Some were merely unstaffed halts, often with just a small platform for one or two carriages and, if you were lucky, a rudimentary shelter and a single lamp. Halts were a comparatively late development for Britain's railways, being pioneered by the Great Western Railway (GWR) on its loss-making branches in the early decades of the 20th century.

At the heart of country life

Country stations were the subject of great local pride. Many companies ran best-kept-station competitions, while some newspapers even ran national ones. Annoyingly for the media, though, it was often the same sites that won each year: stations such as Brough in Yorkshire on the North Eastern Railway (NER), Fleetwood (Fig 3.1) on the Lancashire and Yorkshire, Matlock Bath (Fig 3.2) on the Midland, and Torquay on the GWR.

Fig 3.1 (below)
Fleetwood Station,
Lancashire.
(RO/03704/004)

Fig 3.2 (bottom)
Matlock Bath, Derbyshire.
(RO/002127/002)

Along with the village pub and the village church, the country station also formed one of the principal hubs of the community, providing a social lifeline and an architectural focus for the village. David St John Thomas celebrated the country station as ...

the storeplace for every kind of commodity ... [and] the place where news came from the outside world ... where every piece of invention of the Victorian age could first be seen – from the railway's own telegraph instrument and signaling system ... to threshing machines, mangles, toilet cisterns and bicycles.[3]

As we have seen, from *c* 1850 stations provided the crucial reference points for Greenwich Mean Time, and constituted both the primary telegraphic as well as transport link with the outside world. Local communities bought their newspapers – and milk – from the country station. Indeed, in some rural areas, the station was also where milk was sent: as St John Thomas observed, 'Within weeks of opening, milk churns would be despatched from most country stations; the value of milk to the farmer depended on how far he was from a station.'[4] Locals even used the station as a library, with station bookstalls helping to spread the practice of reading in the Victorian era. By 1860, most stations of any size possessed a lending library, and larger stations even provided Bibles – usually chained to a pillar or a wall, so the more zealous passengers would not take them away with them. At Hawes Junction (now renamed Garsdale: the branch to Hawes was closed in 1959), there was a library in the ladies' waiting room built from an original donation by two elderly ladies of 150 books.

Not every country station was necessarily at the physical heart of the community, however. To save money in hillier regions, many railway companies built their stations in convenient valleys some distance away from the village or town they allegedly served, saving them the expense of creating expensive cuttings and tunnels, as well as building gradients which would subsequently consume much valuable coal. As a result, as David St John Thomas has pointed out concerning the Devon rural railway system, 'hilltop towns like Torrington and South Molton in Devon had their stations in the valley, a mile or so away'.[5] Some were even further away than a mere mile. Those stations which included the qualifier 'Road' in their title were inevitably some distance from their purported destination – certainly a lengthy carriage ride and an even longer walk. Edward Watkin's Metropolitan Railway was a particularly frequent offender in this regard. The Met stations of Chalfont Road, Quainton Road (Fig 3.3), Granborough Road and Winslow Road, for example, were all between one and three miles from the villages and towns they advertised. Not only did this limit traffic after the sites opened; when the 'Beeching Axe' was poised to fall in the 1960s, such remote stations were easy meat for the cost-cutters.

In some rural locations, powerful local landowners kept the station, or indeed the whole line, well away from their estates – and thus from the town the railway company had hoped to reach. Lord Exeter, for example, ensured that the Great Northern Railway (GNR) avoided Stamford and, instead, travelled through Peterborough. This had the predictable result of jump-starting Peterborough's industrial advance and, at the same time, of causing Stamford's economic fossilisation during the second half of the 19th century. It was also to be the unforeseen consequence of the town's success as a major tourist destination in the later 20th century, on account of its charmingly unmodernised Georgian streets. In Sussex, similar machinations by Lord Egremont ensured that, when the London, Brighton and South Coast Railway's (LBSCR) Petworth Station (Fig 3.4) opened in 1859, it was sited almost two miles from the town it had hoped to serve.

Bodmin was the most important town in Cornwall when the Cornwall Railway opened, in that same year of 1859. But the town remained miles away from the railway for two reasons: neither the civic leaders nor the railway could raise sufficient funds to build a branch to the town centre, while local landowner Lord Vivian refused to allow the construction of a

Fig 3.3
Rural isolation: the Metropolitan Railway's optimistically sited station of Quainton Road, Buckinghamshire. Metropolitan it wasn't. (RO/007401/002)

station on his estate. Instead, a station optimistically called Bodmin Road was opened on the new main line to Truro, almost three miles away. It was not until 1887 that the GWR opened Bodmin General Station in the heart of the town. Bodmin General closed in 1967 but, in 1990, reopened as the terminus of the steam-operated Bodmin and Wenford Railway; while Bodmin Road itself was, in 1983, renamed Bodmin Parkway in a conscious (if irony-free) revival of the Victorian 'Road' concept.

Country life

Early permanent stations, as we have seen, were designed in a pleasing variety of architectural styles, from neo-baroque to Tudoresque. From the 1850s, however, railway companies began not just to employ in-house station architects but also to impose standardised designs for many of their smaller stations. Inevitably, as these stations were built of local materials, the designs changed perceptibly as the materials did. Yet the fact that the national spread of the railways made brick available in every area of the country, and not just in the traditional brick-making regions, meant that, even in the north and the west, cheap brick was substituted for local stone in the rush for cost-cutting and consistency.

Many of these country stations, designed by railway architect's offices, are also hard to ascribe to a particular hand. This does not make them necessarily less successful or significant as buildings, however. For example, the delightful cottage orné at Fenny Stratford of 1846 – now empty and deteriorating – was undoubtedly small, but at the same time was attractive, novel and functional. Its first floor daringly jettied out over the platform and, unusually

for the 1840s, the design made a feature of its exposed timber framing – a practice echoed in its cousins further down the Bletchley–Bedford section of the London and Birmingham Railway's (L&BR) long-defunct 'Varsity Line' at Millbrook and Woburn Sands. In a similar vein, the deliciously named Privett Station (Fig 3.5) on the Meon Valley line of the London and South Western Railway (LSWR), built in 1903, was every bit as much of an architectural jewel as some of the largest termini, being devised as a charmingly asymmetrical Tudor house, complete with Tudor-style grid windows for the stationmaster's residence. The up platform was closed as early as 1921, and the whole line in 1955; today the station building is, predictably, a private house.

Some country stations were built, or rebuilt, to reflect their roles as important junctions for branch lines that have now long disappeared. The GWR's Kemble Station was reconfigured

Fig 3.4
Petworth Station, Sussex, in 1892.
(Photograph provided by The Old Railway Station www.old-station.co.uk)

Fig 3.5
Privett, Hampshire, of 1903, in its brief heyday.
(RO/021744/001)

in 1882 in a triangular plan to accommodate the new Cirencester branch, closed in 1964. Today the fine, original stone entrance at Kemble, designed by the GWR in a Late Gothic style which echoes the area's own late-medieval architectural heritage, still survives, though it is many years since it has been in use. The branch's destination, Cirencester Town (Fig 3.6) – a fine, two-storey building of 1841–3 by Brunel and his assistant R P Brereton– also stands, though even by the time it closed in 1964 its Tudor details had already been marred by insensitive remodelling of the late 1950s, which added a clumsy, single-storey extension.

The former station now lies stranded in the middle of a car park in the centre of town, its goods shed, engine shed, cattle pens, a wagon loading bay, four storage sidings and its 'pig wharf' having all long since gone.

Further south, the GWR's post-Brunel station at Faringdon, at the end of a short branch line from the main line at Uffington, was unusual in that its chalet-style main building, with its robust arched openings, was topped by a double hipped roof with a massive chimneystack in the valley gutter. Again, though, the project architect is unknown. The station (Fig 3.7) was closed to passengers as early as

Fig 3.6
The former Cirencester Town Station in the early 1980s.
(BB038281)

Fig 3.7
Faringdon Station shortly before closure in 1951.
(RO/007308/001)

1951, although freight traffic continued to use the branch until 1964 – exactly a century after Faringdon station was so confidently opened. A proposal in 2005 to reopen the line came to nothing, and the building is now in use as a children's nursery.

The survival of the station at Faringdon – at the end of a small branch line which never really recouped its construction and operation costs – was unusual: many rural branches were not so fortunate in the post-war era. Some country stations have, however, managed to survive because of their imaginative reuse, or through their historical associations. The half-timbered elevations of Wolferton in Norfolk of 1898 (Fig 3.8), which improved on a simpler timber station of the early 1860s, were erected to welcome the royal inhabitants of the nearby Sandringham estate, which the Prince of Wales (later King Edward VII) had bought in 1862. This time we do know who designed the building: the remarkably eclectic architect W N Ashbee, head of the Great Eastern Railway's (GER) architectural department between 1883 and 1916. Ashbee appears to have been equally happy with the Continental Baroque of Colchester (1896), the jaunty, tongue-in-cheek Tudorbethan of Felixstowe (1898) and Hertford East (1888), and the domestically scaled, Arts and Crafts lines of Southend Victoria (1889). At Wolferton, Ashbee provided a suite of black-and-white royal reception and retiring rooms, whose projecting gabled roof was supported by brackets carved with large Tudor roses, and a German-looking clock tower. Inside the royal suite could be found Tudor-style linenfold oak panelling, the Prince of Wales's feathers and motto reproduced in plasterwork, a plaster frieze with Tudor roses and flowers, and panelled doors with gold-plated fittings. The station's facilities also included a spacious carriage dock, an ornate building for goods and coal storage, and a small gasworks which lit the entire station. Yet, aside from the Sandringham estate itself, Wolferton served a sparsely populated area – in 1901 the population in the nearby village was 234 souls – and was never busy except for royal parties. Only 645 royal trains terminated there between 1884 and 1911. Departing from Wolferton after a royal birthday party in 1886, it was found that one of the circus elephants could not be loaded onto the train. The animal was tied to a lamppost which it promptly uprooted, and demolished the station gates before calmly boarding its designated truck. At the other end of the animal kingdom, the body of King George VI, who died at Sandringham, was carried by funeral train from Wolferton in February 1952. But by the time the last royal train called at the station in 1966, British Rail was petitioning for its closure – a process which necessitated a formal consultation with the Queen. After HMQ had politely declined to buy the station, it was sold to railwayman Eric Walker, who reopened the royal waiting room in 1970 as a museum

Fig 3.8
The royal station at
Wolferton in Norfolk,
rebuilt in 1898 by W N
Ashbee to serve the Prince
of Wales's retreat at nearby
Sandringham.
(RO/07380/004)

Fig 3.9
Dorking Town (formerly
Dorking West), unforgivably
demolished in the late
1960s.
(OP01430)

to display his collection of royal and historical memorabilia. Walker died in 1985 and his son sought to sell the property. In 1990 the station's contents were auctioned and, in 2001, the station itself was sold to be converted for use as a private house and a small museum.

Outside the pardonably individualistic excesses of royal stations, some railway companies soon learned to impose recognisable house styles. The South Eastern Railway (SER) plumped for domestically scaled brick stations with tall, asymmetric gables, elaborately fretted bargeboards, large dormer windows, tile-clad and jettied first floors and large, powerful chimneystacks. The pattern was established at Chilworth of 1849 (now marred by insensitive window replacements) and at the SER's Redhill–Guildford line stations of 1849–50, the best example of which was at Dorking Town (now Dorking West: Fig 3.9) – a handsome assembly which was disgracefully demolished after 1967. A similar style was repeated at most SER stations of the 1850s: sites such as Crowthorne (originally called Wellington College), whose principal building is now in commercial use; Wye, whose platforms are now connected by a 1930s concrete

footbridge (produced by the Southern Railway concrete factory at Exmouth Junction), and which boasts a window sited in one of the two anchoring chimneystacks; and Grove Ferry and Upstreet in Kent, sadly demolished after closure in 1966. Aylesford, of 1856, was recognisably an SER station, but was particularly individual, with hexagonally glazed metal casement windows, randomly dressed stone walls with ashlar quoins and surrounds, and prominent chimneystacks at either end, set at 45 degrees. The ticket office was closed in September 1989 and an Indian restaurant was subsequently established in the building. Its contemporary cousin at Wateringbury was based on a similar design, this time executed predominantly in brick.

Not every SER station of the 1850s was built to the same approximate formula, however. Snodland of 1856 – a handsome, four-bay classical brick villa with deep, bracketed eaves and with double relieving arches around the round-headed sash windows on the ground floor – was markedly different from the SER norm. And it still survives today, although the first-floor brick elevations have, inexplicably, been painted. So does the long, low building at North Camp of 1863, with its two projecting wings, fine contrasts between yellow stock and red gauged bricks (including rubbed-brick window arches and vertical wall panels) and paired-bracketed eaves, and the station at Bat and Ball (named after a long-defunct pub) at Sevenoaks in Kent, of 1862, which features two large pedimented pavilions connected by single-storey offices. The handsome, six-bay brick baroque villa of St Leonard's Warrior Square in East Sussex is a particularly robust example of the SER's architectural pretensions – even though it commits the architectural solecism of bisecting the broken pediment with a central pilaster. Its Italian-inflected brick front of 1851 demonstrated that the SER's architect William Tress was capable of a wide variety of idioms, and makes a dramatic contrast with the compact power of his Gothic station further up the line at Battle. Tress's eclectic draughtsmanship could encompass everything from neo-baroque to full-blooded Italianate to Tudor; it was, then, perhaps a little unfair for Biddle to castigate his enthusiastically Tudoresque composition at Etchingham (Fig 3.10), also of 1851, as 'an unhappily vague, unrelated Tudorish assemblage'.[6]

Oddly enough, the SER's bitter rival, the London, Chatham and Dover Railway (LCDR), often used a vertically emphasised, domestically inflected Tudor idiom which was clearly derived from that of its principal competitor – building in brick where it could afford to, since the LCDR was always teetering on the brink of bankruptcy.

Repeating gabled dormers, cross-framed 'Tudor' casements, decorative bargeboards and emphatic chimneystacks appear at West Malling, Kent, of 1874 and Wrotham and Borough Green of 1880. On the Ashford–Maidstone line of 1884 – at Lenham (Fig 3.11), Charing and Hollingbourne – the LCDR tended to pursue a format of brick-built stations with a two-storey gabled stationmaster's house connected to single-storey gabled offices with a long, single-storey entrance and waiting room, on either side of which projected awnings for the platform and porch.

Fig 3.10
William Tress's Etchingham, Surrey.
(OP01431)

Fig 3.11
Lenham, Kent, in the 1950s.
(RO/06922/002)

Fig 3.12
Queenborough on the Isle
of Sheppey, Kent, pictured
shortly before demolition
in 1969.
(AA079775)

Some LCDR stations, though, were simply bizarre. The LCDR station at Queenborough on the Isle of Sheppey (Fig 3.12), built in 1860, looked like a witch's castle, with its three steep gables on both entrance and platform elevations and its paired round-arched windows surmounted by giant brick arches. The same concept of three gables gathered on the same elevation, below which relieving arches were placed over paired round-headed windows, also appeared in the same company's stocky head-building at Sheerness Dockyard Station, an uncompromising composition entered through a three-light Venetian opening under a large relieving arch. (The station was closed to passengers as early as 1922, although the building lingered on in increasing dereliction until 1969.) The elevations of both LCDR stations were uncannily similar to that of Lymington Town (Fig 3.13), of 1856–8, for the Lymington Railway (bought by the LSWR in 1879). Both the Lymington branch and the Sheppey lines were overseen by engineer John Cass Birkinshaw, which suggests that he was the primary influence on the rather striking, if somewhat amateur, designs.

When building its line from Leatherhead in Surrey south towards Horsham in Sussex in the mid-1860s, the LBSCR chose a rather more experienced architect than Birkinshaw. The designer of the pyramidal-topped, Teutonic-Romanesque tower at Leatherhead, the gabled porch with the stubby Venetian columns at Boxhill and Westhumble (Fig 3.14), and the bargeboarded brick gables of the now-demolished Dorking North, all of 1867, was architect Charles Driver (1832–1900). Driver had advised Joseph Paxton on casting ornamental ironwork for the Crystal Palace of 1851, had worked with Joseph Bazalgette on London's sewerage system, had built seaside piers from Nice to Llandudno, had assisted R J Hood on stations for the LBSCR, and went on to build a wide-ranging and lucrative practice (leaving an estate of one million pounds on his death), which culminated in his design of the astonishing 'Station of Light' at Sao Paulo, Brazil, of 1897–1900. At the Midland

Fig 3.13
Lymington Town in
Hampshire, of 1856–8.
(Taken from David A
Ingham collection, original
photographer unknown)

Fig 3.14
Charles Driver's exuberantly Gothic station of 1867 at Boxhill and Westhumble, Surrey.
(OP01415)

Railway station at Glendon and Rushton in Northamptonshire (Fig 3.15), of 1857, Driver had introduced elements which were later to be familiar in his Surrey stations: a steeply pitched, two-storey station house with extravagantly decorated bargeboards on all three gable ends. Here, though, Driver also used coupled, round-headed 'neo-Norman' windows with curious hexagonal glazing. A century after it had been built to Driver's design, Glendon and Rushton inevitably fell foul of post-war rationalisation even before Beeching's axe fell, closing in 1960. The building was listed in 1981, and the family of the last stationmaster continued to occupy the building as statutory tenants; however, as it had not been maintained since 1960, the

Fig 3.15
Driver's Glendon and Rushton Station, Northamptonshire: closed in 1960, shortly after this picture was taken, the station is now being lovingly restored.
(RO/17264/002)

fabric of the building soon started to crumble. In 2006, the last member of the Beswick family moved out, leaving the property vacant, and while a series of developers vowed to convert the site into residential properties, they were either denied planning permission or were frustrated by the recession. Finally, in 2011 a group of local volunteers – the Friends of Glendon and Rushton Station, formed two years before – launched a £500,000 fundraising campaign to restore the waiting rooms and booking office to their original condition. They thereby recreated the Victorian railway station, to which they then added museum display areas, a café and a shop.

Back on the south coast, diversity was king. The LBSCR's Cocking of 1881 (closed in 1953, but surviving as a private home) included pargeted plasterwork, half-timbering and a bold oriel window straight out of a Kensington mansion. The same company's Hever of 1888 (Fig 3.16), featuring heavily corniced gabled pavilions, survives as trackside offices. Further east, its low, brick-built stations at Lewes (1889) and Bexhill (1901) both included prominent balustrades with oversized finials and high, top-lit clerestories.

In marked contrast to the LBSCR's East Sussex heterogeneity, the LSWR's larger stations of the 1860s tended to follow the rather more sober example set by Sir William Tite, using as their template a handsome, two-storey, seven-bay 'Georgian' block in a restrained, domestic idiom derived from Tite's Eastleigh of 1839 – though stations such as Netley in Hampshire of 1867, with its projecting, two-bay end pavilions, emphasised quoins, Italianate overhanging eaves and heavy window surrounds, were no doubt rather more elaborate than Tite would have preferred. In the event, the LBSCR was happy to follow this architectural pattern when building its new, coast stations in West Sussex. Hove (originally named Cliftonville, and rebuilt in 1865), and later sites such as Portslade (1881) and West Worthing (1889), were phrased in the same, restrained, Italianate domestic style, adopting the by-now familiar formula of two projecting pavilions at either end of the domestically detailed façade. The same, sensible plan of two taller end pavilions, housing living accommodation or offices, flanking a lower central block comprising the booking hall, waiting room and (if deemed necessary) other services, was inevitably borrowed by other railway companies, too. The GER used it at Long Melford (Fig 3.17), which survives as a private home, and Ongar (Fig 3.18), both of 1865. Indeed the Epping–Ongar Railway is, at time of writing, refurbishing the now privately owned Ongar Station in its original GER corporate colours.

By the 1880s, however, the LSWR had discarded the domestic Georgian and Tudor styles pioneered by William Tite and had settled on a vaguely Dutch house style comprising brick elevations, doubled sashes and high, pedimented gables. The results of this volte-face were seen at Brookwood (an early LSWR example of 1864), Worplesdon of 1883 and New Milton of 1886, all of which were provided with high, pedimented, asymmetric Jacobethan brick gables in the best Dutch manner. Worplesdon

Fig 3.17
Long Melford, Suffolk.
(RO/05850/001)

Fig 3.18
Ongar Station in GER days, before the arrival of LondonTransport.
(RO/07152/001)

Fig 3.19
Corfe Castle, Dorset.
(RO/06758/001)

was later augmented by a delightful, Wrennian entrance pavilion featuring a steeply pitched roof punctuated by a large dormer of doubled windows with a semicircular 'pediment'. At Corfe Castle in 1885, however, the LSWR architects temporarily abandoned any standard approach and built a large terminus in stone in the form of a gabled Gothic station house with doubled and tripled sashes (all with multi-pane upper frames) and a single-storey, dormered entrance pavilion (Fig 3.19).

The Midland Railway's country stations, like those of the SER, were remarkable for their elaborate bargeboards – most notably at stations such as Thurgarton, Nottinghamshire, of

1846. The Midland also invested in elaborate iron awnings, with large, profusely decorated brackets, as at Melton Mowbray (added in 1860 to a station built 20 years previously), Kettering of 1857 (by C H Driver: *see* Fig 1.14) and Keighley and Skipton, both of 1876. At Collingham in 1846 (Fig 3.20), the Midland went further and built a substantial brick villa with a wide-eaved, pedimented projection and flanking arcades.

Buxton Station in Derbyshire was, though, a special case. It originally comprised two linked trainsheds, for the Midland and the LNWR – both lines having arrived in the town in the same year, 1863. The huge lunette at the end of

Fig 3.20
The Midland Railway's
Collingham Station,
Nottinghamshire, of 1846.
(RO/17401/001)

the LNWR's side of the station still survives, set within a massive pedimented gable (Fig 3.21). Gordon Biddle has wondered whether Joseph Paxton had influenced the design for the paired, glazed lunettes. Certainly Paxton had been employed at nearby Chatsworth by the Duke of Devonshire until 1858 and, in 1863, was a still a director of the Midland Railway. Yet, whoever was the author of the design, the station's fine overall roof disappeared as early as the 1920s, and the rest of the station – including all of the Midland's side – was dismantled in 1969.

Standardisation ruled – to a point – on the Midland's Settle–Carlisle line. Built as the company's riposte to the LNWR and Great Eastern's London–Scotland routes, the line was extremely costly to build and never made a profit. But the Midlands refused to skimp on the stations built en route in the middle 1870s. All were well appointed, and characterised by strong, sturdy buildings with large, Tudoresque windows, assertive gable ends, elaborately decorated bargeboards and, at the larger sites, finely bracketed glass-and-iron platform awnings. Interestingly, the Great Central's more northerly stations, such as Sankey, Cheshire, and Widnes North, Lancashire – both of 1873 – and Conisborough and Woodhouse, both in Yorkshire and both of 1884, conformed to the same basic pattern, generally featuring two gabled pavilions with fine, prominent bargeboards bookending a single-storey booking hall. At the Great Central Railway's (GCR) Flixton in Cheshire – built in 1873 for the GCR's ances-

tor, the Manchester, Sheffield and Lincolnshire Railway (MSLR) – the carpenters excelled themselves to produce eccentric, cross-framed bargeboards on both entrance and platform elevations. Tragically, Flixton's fine building, having been converted into a pub, was demolished after a fire of 1997. Thankfully, the equally demonstrative bargeboards at Cressington (Fig 3.22), also of 1873, and complete with elegant Gothic tracery, still remain.

Many country stations, of course – particularly those built for the smaller railways – followed no house style at all. They represent one of the great architectural joys of the countryside – a pleasure that is, today, often

Fig 3.21
The remains of the astonishing station at Buxton in Derbyshire.
(AA98/05410)

Fig 3.22
Cressington, Lancashire.
(RO/04592/001)

Fig 3.23
Richard Whittall's station at
Kenley, with its distinctive,
steeply pitched roofs.
(RO/22280/001)

tinged with sadness, since most of these rural buildings have lost their original function.

Kenley in Surrey (now part of the London Borough of Croydon), built in 1856 for the Caterham Railway by local architect Richard Whittall – who declared it had been designed in the 'Old English style of Domestic Architecture' – boasted an unusual, T-shaped plan, with a large projecting porch and a very steeply pitched roof (Fig 3.23) on shaped wooden posts, whose gable was decorated by mock timber framing with render infill. At the GER's Somerleyton in Suffolk, of 1843, the fabulously wealthy railway contractor Sir Morton Peto hired the sculptor John Thomas to build him not just a vast Jacobethan house (along with an absurdly picturesque, half-timbered and thatched estate village down the road), but also a railway station on the Norfolk Railway (in 1847) which matched his new hall. The sta-

Fig 3.24
Somerleyton Station,
Suffolk, in the 1950s.
(RO/08100/001)

tion (Fig 3.24), which even carried Peto's coat of arms, was built in an engaging Tudor Domestic style which was rather more restrained than the exuberant façades of nearby Somerleyton Hall. Disappointingly, Thomas's highly original design was later ruined by the addition of an ungainly house-tower.

John Thomas (1813–62) was effectively the principal sculptor for the early railway companies. An orphan at 13, he was apprenticed to a stonemason, and subsequently came to the attention of architect Sir Charles Barry – who, to general amazement, hired Thomas to supervise all of the stone-carving in his new Palace of Westminster after 1838. During the 1840s Thomas carved a series of civic coats of arms for the new stations being built on George Stephenson's North Midland Railway (NMR), at the same time as he was commissioned by the Prince Consort to execute large reliefs of 'Peace' and 'War' for Buckingham Palace and by the LNWR to create reliefs depicting the railway's principal destinations and 'Britannia Supported by Science and Industry' for the Great Hall of Euston Station. After 1850,

the tireless Thomas provided the decorative sculpture for Tite's Windsor and Eton Riverside Station and the sculptural group in the pediment at P C Hardwick's Great Western Royal Hotel at Paddington, along with numerous civic and privately commissioned statues and sculptural groups. His involvement at Somerleyton encouraged him to branch out into architecture, and he went on to design the Royal Dairy in Windsor Great Park and Headington Hill House in Oxford.

As we have seen, a free-spirited, light-hearted 'Tudor' was all the rage for stations of the 1840s; and this fashion spread even to the smallest lines. The station at Maldon East and Heybridge (Fig 3.25) was built by Weightman and Hadfield of Sheffield for the Eastern Counties Railway (ECR) between 1846 and 1848. It was a spectacular Tudorbethan brick building, with two pavilions surmounted by Dutch gables, soaring tripled chimneystacks, and a nine-bay arcade masking the entrance front. It was closed in 1964, but now survives as offices. The same firm's Louth in Lincolnshire (of 1848), for the East Lincolnshire Railway (ELR),

Fig 3.25
Maldon East and Heybridge, Essex.
(BB72/03745)

was an even more ambitious Tudorist scheme (Figs 3.26 and 3.27). Its red brick Dutch gables, its steep-pitched, balustraded roof with ball-finials and its imposing, three-bay porte cochère made it, in Biddle's words, 'quite the most handsome station on the Great Northern Railway'[7] (of which the ELR was effectively a part). Although some of the tall chimneystacks have since been removed, marring the overall composition, the lofty and cylindrical central chimneystack still pops out incongruously from behind the middle gable, which is punctuated by an *oeil-de-boeuf* window. The station closed in 1970; having been since converted to

Fig 3.26
Louth, Lincolnshire, in its heyday.
(RO/017158/001)

Fig 3.27
Louth Station during conversion in the 1980s.
(BB94/19342)

residential use, it therefore cannot be used as part of the Lincolnshire Wold Railway's current plans to return railway operation to the picturesque town of Louth.

Some country stations were wholly unique. Matlock Bath, opened in 1849 by the Manchester, Buxton, Matlock and Midland Junction Railway (which was effectively absorbed by the Midland in 1852), was built in an eccentric, 'Swiss chalet' style in an attempt to bolster the town's new campaign to promote itself as 'Little Switzerland'. In the 1890s, Britain's first Alpine-style cable car was even introduced, to take tourists from the station to the natural attraction of the Heights of Abraham. The station itself was timber-framed (the woodwork is now painted an attractive shade of green) with herringbone brick panels, massively overhanging, bracketed eaves, and emphatic, pedimented chimneystacks. The station is no longer in railway use, but is currently in fine condition, and the Derwent Valley Line still operates from the platform.

The station at Chappel and Wakes Colne in Essex (Fig 3.28) was almost as unconventional. The line was built in 1847 by the Stour Valley Railway, incorporated into the ECR in 1854 and then the GER in 1862. While Beeching earmarked the whole of the route for closure, the Marks Tey–Sudbury rump – which is today marketed as 'The Gainsborough Line' – was reprieved in 1966. The rebuilt station of c 1890 at Chappel and Wakes Colne provided passenger access to the raised line via an imposingly high ground floor fronted by a double set of unapologetically steep steps. The fine Edwardian fenestration – sashes with multi-pane frames above and clear plate-glass frames below – was marked with prominent brick keystones linked by terracotta swags, while the verticality of the building was given further emphasis by the unduly tall, quadrupled chimneystacks at either end of the main block. Trains still call here, but in 1987 the station was bought by the enthusiast-run East Anglian Railway Museum.

Fig 3.28
Chappel and Wakes Colne, Essex.
(© Ashley Dace)

While many stations were happy to experiment with an innovative Tudorbethan idiom during the 1840s and 50s, no designer went as far as William Hurst in his splendid station at Stamford East of 1856 (Fig 3.29). Here, Hurst created a stone-fronted Jacobethan mansion with giant Dutch gables and a hugely imposing, turreted and balustraded single-arch entrance. Looking far more like an aristocratic seat than a rural railway terminus, the station was built as the headquarters of the tiny Stamford and Essendine Railway, which was largely worked (and in 1892 leased) by the GNR. The tall booking hall was top-lit by a lantern and ringed by a wrought-iron balustrade gallery, which gave access to the company's offices. Closed in 1957, Hurst's station survives as the private house which it always resembled. With Sancton Wood's astonishing Gothic complex for the Syston and Peterborough Railway, Stamford Town, still in operation close by, the historic jewel that is the ancient town of Stamford thus retains two of the finest mid-sized station buildings in the country.

Gothic enthusiasm was also evident in the astonishingly tall Gothic gables at Needham and Thurston, both built for the Ipswich and Bury Railway after 1846 by the Ipswich-based architect Frederick Barnes, whom we have already met. Thurston fused Tudor and baroque in a very individual manner. Three-storeyed, gabled towers – each punctuated by a tall, round-headed window and an *oeil-de-boeuf* – guarded a recessed block lit with a vast Tudor grid window (above) and a large lunette (below), and topped with a steep pyramidal roof. Between the two towers stretched a triple-arched brick entrance porch which seemed to owe a little to Wren's Temple Bar, its shouldered segmental cornice following the radius of the central arch below. The whole ensemble was saved from looking too top-heavy by the provision of two-storey wings at either side. Although today the station building is privately occupied, the platform, with its scalloped and valanced canopy cantilevered on cast-iron columns, remains in use – a testimony to the days when station architecture was both daring and fun.

Fig 3.29
William Hurst's splendid station at Stamford East, closed in 1957, photographed in the mid-1970s (spot the Austin Allegro) before conversion to residential use. (BB91/24529)

4

The urban station

While architects of country stations such as William Hurst and Frederick Barnes were able to indulge in humorously eclectic flights of fancy, stations in the larger towns and cities were supposed to reflect a seriousness of purpose – and to accommodate a far wider range of functions and services – than their smaller country cousins.

Restrained classicism

The earliest urban stations, as we have seen, were designed so as to frighten neither the horses nor potential passengers. Thus George Smith's Greenwich of 1840 was built to look like a seven-bay mansion (Fig 4.1). Erected of yellow London stock brick, with a stone frieze and deeply eaved cornice, stone architraves for the

windows and a doorcase flanked by attached Ionic columns, it had little in common with the recognisably 'railway' architecture that was to follow. Smith (1782–1869) had worked in the offices of James Wyatt and Daniel Alexander and was subsequently employed as a surveyor to the City of London and to the Mercers and Coopers Companies. In 1844 he was appointed one of the vice-presidents of the new Institute of British Architects. Sir Howard Colvin described him in terms which could also be applied to his Greenwich Station: 'a careful and meticulous man whose office was a model of orderliness'.[1]

The restrained, domestic and sedately classical pattern set by Smith's Greenwich and William Tite's early, classical London and South Western Railway (LSWR) stations was frequently reused in urban contexts across

Fig 4.1
Railway domestic:
Greenwich Station of 1840.
(© 2008 Sunil060902, used
under a Creative Commons
Attribution-ShareAlike
licence:
http://creativecommons.
org/licences/by-sa/3.0/.
Taken from
http://en.wikipedia.org/
wiki/Greenwich_station)

England. Most, though, followed Tite's formula of projecting the outermost bays, so that the resulting composition looked less like a country house and more like an urban villa. At Gravesend in Kent, built in 1849 for the South Eastern Railway (SER), a Tuscan colonnade was inserted between the two projecting pavilions and the ground-floor windows on the latter enlarged into three-light compositions with heavy stone surrounds. As noted above, all of the London, Brighton and South Coast Railway's (LBSCR) stations along the railway's south coast line – from Seaford in East Sussex (where the walls were rendered) to Arundel in West Sussex (where they were left as plain brick) – adopted the same basic configuration. Christ's Hospital in West Sussex – built some years later, in 1902, and demolished in 1972 – adapted what had, in the 1860s, been a classical blueprint in the Gothic idiom, with pronounced bargeboards and patterned brickwork adorning the two-bay projections.

Flights of fancy

The 1860s were not just about tasteful classicism, however. Away from the south coast, railway companies now felt confident enough to promote eclecticism and inventiveness. No longer were urban railway stations to be sedate, modest buildings designed to harmonise with the local townscape. Now they could experiment with a bewildering variety of styles and motifs. For example, the delightful brick frontage of Herne Bay in Kent of 1863 – built by the Herne Bay and Faversham Railway Company, which was acquired by the London, Chatham and Dover Railway (LCDR) in 1871 – boasted not one but four triangular pediments, the central two being provided with striated brick arches which, in turn, supported a long, glazed canopy-cum-porte cochère. All these features were punctuated by large, round rosette windows surmounting (in three out of four of the bays) three 'Early English' lancet openings. The buildings on the down platform are all that remain of the original station building; those on the up side were, dispiritingly, reconstructed by the Southern Railway in 1926 as an uninspiring, flat-roofed block, as part of the Southern's interwar plan to modernise the Thanet lines.

At the other end of the country, William Peachey's Saltburn, Yorkshire, of 1861, for the Stockton and Darlington Railway (S&DR), was as demonstrative as Herne Bay. Dominated by its full-height, three-arched porte cochère and its engaging buff bricks with yellow sandstone dressings, the curious glazing pattern of its windows was of the 'Lombardic' type, then very much in fashion. Today, the station building is in retail use, the trainshed has gone, and trains terminate at one meanly equipped platform away from the original site. The wonderfully exuberant and elongated Tudor frontage at Yeovil Town, Somerset, built in 1861 for the Bristol and Exeter Railway – with its odd, five-bay pavilion, with triangular gable behind a steep roof culminating in a large chimney, and two-storey, gabled bookends flanked by thrusting chimneystacks – much in the manner of Frederick Barnes or C H Driver – has also gone, demolished soon after the station's closure in 1967.

One of the most characterful semi-urban stations of the 1860s was E W Elmslie's Gothic masterpiece, Great Malvern in Worcestershire, of 1862 (Fig 4.2). Elmslie had settled in the town around 1854, and soon set up an architectural practice – Elmslie, Franey and Haddon – which set about building some of the growing resort's most impressive public buildings. The station was certainly one of the firm's most accomplished compositions: long and low, with vertical emphases provided by paired chimneys and numerous gables, its deep platform awnings were supported by brackets with ornamental pierced spandrels and iron columns topped by extraordinary, brightly coloured and foliage-strewn capitals wrought by William Forsyth, whom *The Builder* praised in 1863 for having 'cleverly introduced the foliage of the plants of the neighbourhood'.[2]

Other great urban railway monuments of the 1860s are still with us, too. The fine, imposing brick station at Herne Hill in South London, with its squat tower flanking a tall brick block of six bays, dates from 1862 and was built for the LCDR (Fig 4.3). Its height was necessary, as the line was carried on a viaduct at this point, and thus the platforms needed to be at first-floor level. The station was designed by architect John Taylor, and was dominated by its tower – which actually concealed the water tank used for replenishing steam locomotives. *Building News* described the station as 'spacious and convenient … and of the very best quality',[3] which prompted the editor to write a 2,000-word article bemoaning the poor architectural quality of other contemporary civil engineering projects.

Fig 4.2
High Gothic: Great Malvern,
of 1862.
(OP26924)

Fig 4.3
The imposing brick elevation
of Herne Hill.
(© 2012 Tommy20000,
used under a Creative
Commons Attribution-
ShareAlike licence:
http://creativecommons.
org/licences/by-sa/3.0/.
Taken from
http://en.wikipedia.org/
*wiki/Herne_Hill_railway_*
station)

lit booking hall, the doubled columns and the roundels in the arch spandrels were a nod to Sir Christopher Wren, and specifically to the latter's 1672 masterpiece: the church of St Stephen Walbrook. (Though Wren never placed female heads in his circular openings, as the LBSCR's anonymous architect chose to do.) Charles Barry junior's North Dulwich, built for the same company between 1866 and 1868, also cited Wren, featuring a three-bay colonnade with paired Tuscan capitals in Wrennian fashion.

Diversity continued to flourish in the stations of the 1870s. E H Horne used Venetian Gothic for his North London Railway stations sited between Camden Road (originally Camden Town) and Bow. Camden, of 1870 and of yellow brick with stone dressings is the only survivor. Its paired, round-headed windows were provided with relieving arches on the first floor and arranged as single compositions of 'Lombardic' neo-Romanesque tracery, in the manner of Peachey's Saltburn. Paley and Austin's Ulverston, Cumbria, built in 1873 for the Furness Railway, had a tall, church-like tower which originally presided over delicate glazed iron awnings. The LBSCR's fine classical station at Crystal Palace Low Level in South London of 1875 (Fig 4.5), built to cope with the crowds of visitors to the Crystal Palace, which was relocated here from Hyde Park in 1854, featured paired windows of a highly original design. Its fine porte cochère has gone, and the new ironwork merely crudely mimics what has disappeared, but the fine, high interior is now reopened, thanks to the arrival of the London

Fig 4.4 (above)
Battersea Park, of 1867.
(© 2008 Sunil060902, used under a Creative Commons Attribution-ShareAlike licence:
http://creativecommons. org/licences/by-sa/3.0/. Taken from
http://en.wikipedia.org/ wiki/Battersea_Park_ railway_station)

Even more forbidding, but highly appropriate for its cramped, urban location, was the LBSCR's exceedingly tall, polychromic elevation at Battersea Park of 1867, comprising a five-bay building sandwiched between two railway bridges (Fig 4.4). In the lofty, lantern-

Fig 4.5 (right)
Crystal Palace Low Level: mutilated in the 1960s, it has recently been restored. (© 2013 SheffGruff, used under a Creative Commons Attribution-ShareAlike licence:
http://creativecommons. org/licences/by-sa/3.0/. Taken from
http://en.wikipedia.org/ wiki/Crystal_Palace_ railway_station)

Overground line from East London. The marvellous Italianate station at Lytham, Lancashire, built in 1874 for the Preston and Wyre Joint Railway (a collaboration between the London and North Western Railway (LNWR) and the Lancashire and Yorkshire Railway), is still with us. Its long, low brick front (its awning porch long gone) in Ballam Road, surmounted by a segmental-pedimented clock, belongs more to Sorrento than to the Fylde. Thankfully, the main station building has survived to be converted into a pub-restaurant in 1986. Sadly, though, the marvellous, transverse glazed platform canopies were removed in the 1960s; all waiting passengers have to keep the rain off now is a tiny plastic bus shelter.

By the 1880s smaller urban stations, like their country cousins, invariably tended to be brick-built. Demark Hill, built in 1886 for the LBSCR

(Fig 4.6), was phrased in a cheerful Italianate style and on a surprisingly large scale. Gutted in a fire of 1980, the main building was rebuilt as a pub. Pedimented Dutch gables were used by the LSWR in their South London stations of Wimbledon Park and East Putney of 1889 (the broken pediment at East Putney even framed a large, oval *oeil-de-boeuf* window), while a distinct Arts and Crafts influence was evident in the LBSCR's large, brick Streatham Common of 1890, where half-timbering is strangely supplemented by large circular windows. Three large gables under a steeply pitched roof each with a large *oeil-de-boeuf* opening at the same company's Thornton Heath (Fig 4.7), rebuilt in 1903, lent the station an appearance more reminiscent of Cologne than Croydon. Thornton Heath's jaunty central cupola was, though, demolished in the 1970s.

Fig 4.6
Denmark Hill of 1886: reborn, phoenix-like, as a pub.
(RO/22158/002)

Fig 4.7
Thornton Heath of 1903, with its original cupola.
(RO/24059/001)

By the 1880s, too, the Great Western Railway (GWR) had long since abandoned Brunel's Tudorist idiom and, for its larger town stations, was experimenting with a vaguely French Renaissance style, which usually involved the provision of two (or possibly three) projecting, flat-topped pavilions crowned with delicate ironwork. This approach was first used at Truro, Cornwall, and Southall, Middlesex, of 1876; at Stourbridge Town, Worcestershire (Fig 4.8), and Langley, Buckinghamshire, of 1879; and at Ross-on-Wye, Herefordshire, of 1882.

Stourbridge Town was demolished as recently as 1979, exactly a century after its birth. Ross, once an important junction, was inexplicably closed in 1964, while the buildings lingered for over a decade before they were demolished to make way for an industrial estate. The station's design was, however, posthumously revived at Kidderminster Town thanks to the enthusiastic volunteers of the Severn Valley Railway.

However, no GWR station, nor indeed the buildings of any other company, ever looked as authentically French as those at Slough, of

1882–6 (Fig 4.9). This infamous town makes a rather unlikely setting for the Renaissance curves of J E Banks's homage to the Second Empire style. Three big brick pavilions – the central one of two storeys and five bays – were fronted by pilasters rising into attic acroteria and topped with bulbous, curving roofs covered with zinc fish-scale tiles (now replaced by GRP substitutes), punctuated by *oeil-de-boeuf* attic windows (surmounted with William Kent-style scallop shells) and culminating in wrought-iron, balustrade platforms. The central block was dominated by a clock in a broken segmental pediment, topped with a precarious-looking ball finial. The continuous iron canopy in front of central and linking blocks, supported on open, cast-iron brackets, obscured much of the ground floor – but, as Gordon Biddle noted 40 years ago, at Slough 'the icing was all on top with plain cake underneath'.[4]

On occasion, the French influence permeated further afield. Norwich Thorpe's chateau-style confection (now listed Grade II*) was built in 1886 by the Great Eastern Railway's (GER) John Wilson and his architectural assistant W N Ashbee (Fig 4.10). Its four-bay domed centre, topped with a high dome and jaunty lantern (which creates the architectural solecism of a five-pilaster elevation) is flanked by four chimneystacks and fronted by a large clock-gable which looks as if it belongs on a giant's mantelpiece.

GWR's Windsor and Eton Central, impressively rebuilt in 1897 in an attempt to rival Tite's magnificent Riverside Station further north (Fig 4.11), was fronted by a giant, glazed elliptical arch. Inside the generous iron shed – which was never an actual trainshed; the station itself was to the north, while the southern area was occupied by a cab yard – was a stone-faced, single-storey royal waiting room (Fig 4.12), last used in 1936 and now a restaurant, but which still retains some of its original fireplace surrounds and overmantels, and mouldings. In 1982, British Railways leased part of the station area to Madame Tussauds, who created a permanent exhibition adjacent to the one working platform, entitled *Royalty and Railways*, using wax models, animatronic figures and a full-size replica Royal Train. After the failure of the museum, the station and its covered curtilage were largely converted to a shopping complex by DLG Architects of Leeds in 1997. The remaining, single platform was truncated still further, and can now handle no more than a three-car train.

By 1900, all manner of architectural eclecticism was permitted in urban railway stations, as railway companies cast off their stylistic shackles and tentatively experimented with architectural idioms that had long been prevalent in continental Europe and America. At Goodmayes, Essex, of 1900 (Fig 4.13), the

Fig 4.10
Norwich Thorpe: Wilson and Ashbee, 1886.
(© 2005 Bluemoose, used under a Creative Commons Attribution-ShareAlike licence:
http://creativecommons. org/licences/by-sa/3.0/. Taken from
http://en.wikipedia.org/ wiki/Norwich_railway_ station)

Fig 4.11
Windsor & Eton Central:
the dramatic entrance, just
opposite Windsor Castle as
seen in c 1960. The station
survives, albeit largely as
a shopping mall, but the
Thames Valley bus services
have long gone.
(OP26922)

Fig 4.12
Windsor & Eton Central's
trainshed. The royal waiting
room can be seen to the
right.
(OP26921)

GER eschewed the jettied, half-timbered porch gables used elsewhere on the Southend line (at stations such as Wickford, Hockley and Rayleigh, all of 1889) and splashed out on a delightful essay in English baroque. Here the double-doored entrance was surmounted by a large, segmental pediment redolent of Nicholas Hawksmoor. Not to be outdone (as they usually were), the more inescapably suburban London, Tilbury and Southend Railway built an unapologetically baroque entrance to their nearby East Ham Station of 1902, complete with oval window and open pediment.

In 1899 the SER and the LCDR finally buried the hatchet – largely due to the mounting financial pressures on the two perennially cash-strapped operations – and merged as the South Eastern and Chatham Railway (SECR), although both components kept their separate board of directors. The SER had been particularly unpopular with its passengers, who believed that its ebullient chairman, Edward Watkin, was sacrificing the company's financial prospects on the altar of his ambitious Channel Tunnel project. The merger, however, prompted a flurry of station building on the SECR lines, small new stations being added in a transatlantic Beaux Arts classical idiom. They were

mostly executed in brick and characterised by simplified classical details, large, centralised pediments and big lunette (or 'Diocletian') windows in the manner of many American stations of the period. Typical of the new look was the very handsome composition at Tadworth of 1900, comprising a pedimented porch with a large lunette in its pediment flanked by four bay wings terminating in arched doorways.

By 1900, bigger urban stations were allowed to be even more demonstrative. The LBSCR's Bognor Regis of 1902 was a four-square, impressively gabled station building phrased in the manner of a North Oxford villa upon whose steep roof had alighted an oversized, Rhenish clock tower. This design appeared conventional, however, when compared to that of Bexhill West, built in the same year. The SECR's belated branch to Bexhill resulted in perhaps the most continental of all turn-of-the-century stations. At Bexhill West (Fig 4.14), two large gabled pavilions terminated a steeply pitched roof carrying a large clock tower, complete with pilastered supports for both segmental pediments *and* a dome. Below the clock tower, an emphatically broken pediment sat uneasily atop a massive, pilastered brick-and-stone entrance arch behind a steeply

Fig 4.13
Essex Baroque at Goodmayes of 1900. (© 2009 Sunil060902, used under a Creative Commons Attribution-ShareAlike licence: http://creativecommons. org/licences/by-sa/3.0/. Taken from http://en.wikipedia.org/ wiki/Goodmayes_railway_ station)

pedimented entrance. Not to be outdone, the two flanking, half-timbered pavilions contained a large segmental relieving arch over tripled sash windows, whose brick-and-terracotta surrounds culminated in a pedimented cartouche supported by vast, scrolled brackets. This astonishing station was closed in 1964, but reassuringly survives as offices, and was finally listed Grade II in 2013.

Staid, conservative Tunbridge Wells's two stations almost outdid Bexhill West in their unconventionality. The original, upside building at the SER's Central Station was a fine, well-mannered, seven-bay brick pile of 1846, executed in a neat, Georgian domestic style (Fig 4.15). In 1911, however, the ramshackle downside buildings were rebuilt in a far more ambitious, Teutonic style to the design of the normally sober Arthur Blomfield, who excelled himself with two vast lunettes and an imposing if eccentric baroque clock tower which gives the station more grandeur and apparent size than it possesses. Even this composition, however, looked tame when compared to the LBSCR's vast High Gothic extravaganza to the south-west (*see* p 129).

Fig 4.14
Bexhill West of 1902: Germany comes to Sussex. (© 2009 Ravenseft, used under a Creative Commons Attribution-ShareAlike licence: http://creativecommons. org/licences/by-sa/3.0/. Taken from http://en.wikipedia.org/ wiki/Bexhill_West_railway_ station)

Fig 4.15
Tunbridge Wells: the original SER station of 1846. (RO/06987/006)

Nor was outrageous expressionism limited to the south coast. The neo-Norman brick tower at Birkenhead Hamilton Square, of 1898, by G E Grayson, was actually a hydraulic aid – to give the water enough head to operate the hydraulic lifts below to platform level 27m (90ft) underground. And the Midland's new station at Morecambe Promenade of 1907 (Fig 4.16) looked positively Germanic: E G Paley (or possibly Thomas Wheatley) creating a long, low composition in honey-coloured sandstone (rescued by the railway from its former station in Northumberland Street) punctuated with a central, three-bay block set with the pedimented attic clock tower and end gabled pavilions with tripled lancets and *oeil-de-boeuf* openings. In a defeatist blow to the regional economy, in 1994

the local authority closed the station and built a minimalist replacement nearer the town centre. The old station reopened as a restaurant and tourist information centre in 1997.

Miniature urban essays, however, could be just as effective as soaring gestures. The splendid, three-bay brick pavilion with steeply pitched pyramidal roof and baroque cartouche-pediment above the door at Bellingham, Kent, of 1892 remains a delightful jewel. West Kirby in the Wirral of 1896 (Fig 4.17) had a tall, bulky, castellated Arts and Crafts clock tower – with a clock on each face, just in case – in the vein of the influential American architect H H Richardson. The tower sat (and indeed sits) beside two projecting, half-timbered gabled pavilions (whose woodwork is now finished in a fetching

Fig 4.16
Morecambe Promenade Station of 1907 today. (Photograph provided by www.heritagephotoarchive. co.uk)

Fig 4.17
West Kirby, Cheshire, in the early years of the 20th century. (RO/04620/001)

Brunswick green), sandwiching the recessed booking hall. The handsome, seven-bay Queen Anne front of Merstham, Surrey, of 1905 (Fig 4.18), with its central broken pediment and its white-and-terracotta decorative scheme, typified the Edwardian trend to diminution. Best of all the small urban stations of that confident era before the Great War, however, was Gerald Horsley's compact, symmetrical, Wrennian pavilion at the entrance to Hatch End, Middlesex, of 1911 (Fig 4.19). Its main elevation was dominated by two large arches, incorporating both windows and the glazed entrance, beneath big lunette openings. Between the arches was a large, swagged sculptural essay on the LNWR's coat of arms; above perched a pyramidal roof surmounted by pedimented cupola, inset with a clock.

None of these, though, had the swagger and bravura of Southern's Palladian villa at Bromley North, Kent, of 1925 (Fig 4.20). With its vast pedimented entrance bay, set with a giant arched door, and a tall, domed cupola supported on eight wooden Doric columns, it continues to dominate an otherwise architecturally undistinguished high street. Exmouth was rebuilt in the early 1930s by the Southern in a similarly bombastic, neo-baroque manner, with a steeply pitched roof, side bays emphasised with stone facings and a garlanded attic clock. However, this bravura composition was cruelly demolished when the station footprint was dramatically reduced in 1968.

By 1930, the new Southern Railway's chief architect, J R Scott, appeared to have become smitten by both the modernist and art deco

Fig 4.18 (above)
Merstham, Surrey.
(© 2007 Nse1986, used under a Creative Commons Attribution-ShareAlike licence:
http://creativecommons.org/licences/by-sa/3.0/.
Taken from http://en.wikipedia.org/wiki/Merstham_railway_station)

Fig 4.19 (right)
Hatch End, Middlesex.
Horsley's pavilion of 1911 can be seen to the right.
(RO/22248/003)

movements. These influences were craftily fused with the contemporary fashion for stripped classicism (from which the art deco fashion post-1925 had itself derived) to create an idiom ideally suited for everyday use. And while the Southern's larger stations of the 1920s tended to be more conservative, the smaller, suburban buildings they built were often daringly innovative.

James Robb Scott (1882–1965) was born in the Gorbals in Glasgow, the son of an architect. He trained as an architect in Edinburgh and London before joining the LSWR's architectural office in 1907, where he masterminded the architecture of the comprehensive but perennially interrupted rebuilding of Waterloo between 1909 and 1923 (*see* Chapter 5). With the grouping of the railways in 1923, Scott was the obvious choice to become chief architect of the Southern Railway; indeed, he was even able to keep his office in Waterloo.

As chief architect to the Southern Railway, Scott was responsible for the team which rebuilt some of the principal urban stations – Margate, Ramsgate and Hastings – on the Kent and East Sussex coast, as well as the new stations on the newly electrified, former LSWR suburban lines of the 1930s to the South-West London destinations of Kingston, Richmond and beyond. However, the disparity between

the bombastic baroque of the Waterloo Arch – planned before the First World War but not completed until 1922 – and the radical modernism of some of the Southern's suburban stations of 1930–7 has led some historians to suggest that it was not Scott who was responsible for the actual designs but his chief assistant for much of the 1920s: the young Turk, Edwin Maxwell Fry (1899–1987). Fry subsequently became one of the few British architects to enthusiastically embrace modernism and, in later life, tended to elaborate on the account of his time with Southern Railways. The idea that Fry, not Scott, was the real designer of the Southern's radical new stations was inspired by the callous and ungrateful tone of Fry's self-serving autobiography, in which he unprofessionally disparaged Scott as 'a lumbering Scotsman only waiting for the salmon rivers to rise'. Scott, he venomously alleged ...

fell into my hands like a ripe plum as by one of these sudden spurts of decisive action I took over the hotel design that was beyond him, and was installed by the Chief Engineer as his deputy and working factotum ... and I immediately set about reinforcing the time-serving staff of old bodies with all the friends and acquaintances I could lay hold of. There was plenty of work and one by one I signed on an assortment of young men who transformed the place of lingering fears and deceptions...[5]

However, there is no direct evidence to support such allegations, which tend to reflect poorly on Fry's character rather than on Scott's achievements.

Whoever was primarily responsible for their design, the minimalist, modernist-inflected, art deco-styled classicism of the big new seaside stations at Margate (Fig 4.21), Ramsgate (both of 1924–6) and Hastings (of 1931 – four years after Fry had left the Southern) was unmistakeable (Fig 4.22). All three sites – along with many of the intermediate stations, too – had been rebuilt to complement and advertise the new, electrified lines introduced by the Southern's chief engineer, A W Szlumper, in what became one of the biggest civil engineering projects of the interwar years. Over their giant entrance porches, both Margate and Hastings were furnished with single, giant lunette windows – a motif that had become an internationally recognised symbol for the railway station at the turn of the 20th century. At Ramsgate, the palatial booking hall was lit by three, huge, round-arched windows in the manner of a German or American union station, while its east and west walls were decorated with 'Egyptian' motifs – a decorative treatment which had become topically popular after Lord Carnarvon's dis-

Fig 4.21
The Southern's 'Moderne' station at Margate, begun in 1924.
(AA046460)

Fig 4.22
The original Hastings Station of 1931.
(© John Minnis)

covery of the tomb of Tutankhamun in 1922. At Margate, another vast lunette rose from the entrance porch, which was flanked by heavy, projecting, single-bay pavilions and stone Doric pilasters and balanced by long, low wings with large, round-headed windows, while inside was a massive, elliptically vaulted booking hall. Hastings, built five years later, was a simplified version of Margate, with blander wings and the railway's name emblazoned across the massive stone frieze. Astonishingly, though, this fine and important station was demolished with the consent of the local authority in 2004 to make way for a nondescript commercial development – albeit one punctuated by a good modern station.

Ramsgate, Margate and Hastings stations were, it has often been alleged, heavily influenced by the new tube stations for the London Underground then being built by Charles Holden and his colleagues. This influence was still discernible, if less obviously, in the radical, quasi-modernist stations built for the Southern's newly electrified suburban lines in South London and Surrey during the 1930s. Nothing like these stations had been built on the railways before – not even on Holden's Piccadilly or Northern lines. They fused bold, minimally decorated masses of stone or concrete with innovative glazing, using the latest metal windows, and allusions to the heritage of classicism. Richmond (1936), with its projecting, three-bay entrance dominated by rectangular metal fenestration, looked more like the Scan-

dinavian designs which had in turn influenced Holden. Tolworth of 1938 (Fig 4.23), Malden Manor of 1938 (Fig 4.24) and Chessington North of 1939 (Fig 4.25) were particularly original, with a low entrance hall offset by an asymmetrical, blank concrete tower necessary to access the high platforms, whose awnings were of ribbed, cantilevered concrete. The

Fig 4.23 (top)
Tolworth, Surrey, of 1938.
(RO/24060/003)

Fig 4.24 (above)
Malden Manor: Southern Moderne at its most minimal.
(RO/24210/003)

Fig 4.25
Chessington North, as rebuilt in 1939.
(RO/22126/001)

83

entrance to Wimbledon Chase (1929) was simply a massive, curved entablature supported by pillars at either end; Chessington South of 1939 (Fig 4.26), a similar exercise but this time in brick, was even more reticent, relying on the massive, cylindrical pillars at each end of the entrance elevation for its effect. The confident, brick modernism of St Mary Cray of 1938 (Fig 4.27), with its single string course and deep attic decorated only by a bordered row of canted bricks at each corner, was so powerful and bold, but was mutilated beyond recogni-

Fig 4.26
The gaunt brick and concrete of Chessington South Station, of 1939, seen shortly after opening.
(RO/22127/002)

Fig 4.27
St Mary Cray, Kent: now barely recognisable as the bold new station of 1938.
(© 2008 Sunil060902, used under a Creative Commons Attribution-ShareAlike licence:
http://creativecommons.org/licences/by-sa/3.0/. Taken from
http://en.wikipedia.org/wiki/St_Mary_Cray_railway_station)

tion in subsequent years. Happily, in contrast to the miserable fate of St Mary Cray, the Southern's art deco masterpiece at Surbiton of 1937 (was it Scott or was it Fry?) has been superbly restored (Fig 4.28). With its Holdenesque four-bay grid of immensely tall Scandinavian-style windows, its soaring, continental-looking tower and its white plaster walls, it brings a touch of

international glamour to this architecturally commonplace corner of Greater London.

The former LSWR lines did not have a monopoly on Southern moderne. At Durrington in West Sussex, of 1937 (Fig 4.29), a square, Holdenesque tower with flat brick buttresses rises, cathedral-like, from a long, low brick range bolstered by two corner pavilions.

Fig 4.28
Surbiton: the art deco castle in the suburbs.
(© 2012 Ok2010, used under a Creative Commons Attribution-ShareAlike licence:
http://creativecommons.org/licences/by-sa/3.0/.
Taken from http://en.wikipedia.org/wiki/Surbiton_railway_station)

Fig 4.29
The powerful composition of Durrington, West Sussex, of 1937.
(© Kim Rennie)

The remarkable station at Bishopstone, East Sussex, of 1936 (Fig 4.30), now listed, has a large, octagonal clerestory – whose windows light the booking hall below – which rises from a handsome, low, brick building, with wraparound metal windows at its corners, in a manner distinctly reminiscent of Charles Holden's underground stations (*see* p 90). Beneath the octagon, two brick-and-concrete pillboxes were sensitively inserted at 45 degree angles in 1940, just in case the Germans should try to invade Seaford.

The art deco style, though, was sparingly used elsewhere on England's railways. A rare example is Leamington Spa (Fig 4.31), which fuses the entrance front of a large English country house with modish art deco styling. Its author was P A Culverhouse, the GWR's chief architect for most of the interwar years and the man who added the third span to Brunel's Paddington trainshed. Elsewhere, cool neo-Georgian was more popular than any of the moderne styles. The sedate, 'Colonial Revival' station for the London and North Eastern Railway (LNER) at Welwyn Garden City, Hertfordshire, of 1926, with its projecting, tetrastyle Tuscan porch, its large sash windows and its three central dormers, could have been built in Williamsburg, Virginia. Replaced as the city's principal station when the Howard Centre was opened in 1990, the building now serves – very appropriately, given its strong resemblance to an American Colonial Revival bank – as offices. The cliff-like façade of Byfleet and New Haw, Surrey, of 1927, with its massive entrance arch and half-timbered gable, harked back to the 19th century, while the suave classicism of the Southern's Exeter Central of 1933 (Fig 4.32) – very much in the vein of architect Vincent Harris, who was working at Exeter University at the time – was derived from the 18th, although its inspiration was, like that of Welwyn Garden City Station, perhaps more Colonial than Georgian. Exeter Central's tall central block was surmounted by a towering cupola – a feature which, taken together with the choice of

Fig 4.30
Bishopstone, East Sussex, in 1973.
(Taken from David A Ingham collection, original photographer unknown)

Fig 4.31
Leamington Spa: a rare example of an interwar GWR station.
(© David White)

brick for the façade, the projecting five bays and the three large, ground-floor arched windows, made the whole composition look as if it had been plucked from the campuses of Harvard or Yale. The sweeping, two-storey wings that curved westwards confirmed the impression of an American academic institution. (Today, sadly, the miserly entrance to Central Station occupies just a fragment of this grand 1933 façade.) Clacton, Essex, of 1929 for the LNER, was an attempt to fuse a more conservative neo-Georgian style with the art deco bragga-docio of Ramsgate and Margate; but ultimately it fails to do either (Fig 4.33). The stone-clad centrepiece is oddly proportioned, and draws attention not to the station entrance but to a pair of what seem to be kitchen doors stranded halfway up the elevation. At the same time, the rhythm of bays is jarringly uneven, with three on one side and two on the other.

Fig 4.32
Exeter Central Station:
sedate classicism of 1933.
(© Derek Harper)

Fig 4.33
The bizarre station at
Clacton of 1929.
(© Robert Edwards)

Fig 4.34
Croxley, Hertfordshire,
pictured in c 1950.
(RO/06283/001)

Fig 4.35 (above)
The Metropolitan Railway's
Watford Station shortly
after opening. The station
may soon be redundant, but
hopefully this fine station
building will survive.
(Taken from Phil Marsh
collection, original
photographer unknown)

On the Metropolitan Railway in Hertfordshire, architect C W Clark built attractive, vernacular-revival stations at Croxley and Watford in 1925 (Figs 4.34 and 4.35). These were devised as two Voyseyesque compositions with large dormer windows, steeply pitched roofs and emphatic brickstacks. Clark went on to adapt the Croxley and Watford formula for Kingsbury and Stanmore (then part of the Metropolitan Railway, now on London Underground's Jubilee Line) in 1932. He also built the Met's own headquarters of Selbie House in 1913 in a grand, faience-clad neo-baroque style (Fig 4.36). When the Croxley Rail Link is complete in 2016, Clark's fine Arts and Crafts essay at Watford – now, reassuringly, listed Grade II – will, though, be made redundant.

Almost all of the new suburban stations of the 1920s and 30s enjoyed some sort of subsidy from developers. In 1919 the Metropolitan

Railway even set up its own company to promote housing developments within walking or cycling distance of its new stations. The term 'Metro-land' had already been coined by the railway's marketing department in 1915 and, in 1929, Clark's Chiltern Court, a luxurious block of apartments over Baker Street, was launched onto the market. As early as 1903 the Metropolitan developed a housing estate at Cecil Park, Pinner, and thereafter followed with a number of similar developments in north-west London, Hertfordshire and Buckinghamshire. Some new stations, such as Hillingdon of 1923, were built specifically to serve the company's suburban developments. Charles Holden's London Underground stations, however, were built for a very different reason: to provide railway access to the rapidly growing suburbs of what was to become Greater London. The story of their design and construction has often been told, but it is worth bearing in mind just how advanced they were for the time: aside from the Southern's suburban stations of the 1920s and 30s, nothing like them appeared during this period.

Going underground

Charles Holden (1875–1960) was born in Bolton, Lancashire, the fifth child of a draper and milliner. After training in Manchester, though, he moved to London and, following his marriage, to Hertfordshire. He made his name with his designs for the Belgrave Hospital for

Children in Kennington of 1900–3, a composition which betrayed his debt to the Arts and Crafts movement, and the Bristol Central Library of 1902, a fusion of Tudorism and modernism which Pevsner called 'free Neo-Tudor', and which he thought 'extremely pretty'. His practice became Adams, Holden & Pearson in 1913, and the same year he was awarded the RIBA's Godwin Medal. After the First World War he worked for the Imperial War Graves Commission and, through his involvement with the Design and Industries Association, met Frank Pick of the Underground Electric Railways Company (UERC).

Fig 4.36
Selbie House of 1913,
close to the Metropolitan
Railway's Baker Street
terminus.
(AA063062)

In 1924, Pick commissioned Holden to design seven new stations in south London for the extension of the UERC's City and South London Railway, from Clapham Common to Morden. Holden's stations combined stripped or implied classicism with simple modernist forms. His genius was to create surprisingly large spaces – notably his double-height ticket halls – in difficult, cramped locations. At South Wimbledon of 1926 (Fig 4.37), for example, the piers supporting the external awning-porch continued up through the large, glazed grid window above in the form of pilasters, their capitals transformed into a three-dimensional UERC

roundel – a symbol the UERC was already using as its corporate logo and which would be made internationally famous by its successor, London Transport. In 1930 Holden and Pick made a tour of Germany, the Netherlands, Denmark and Sweden to witness at first hand the latest developments in modern architecture, a visit which heavily influenced Holden's subsequent designs for the stations built on the westward and northern extensions of the Piccadilly and District lines for what, in 1933, became the London Transport Board. Holden's first Piccadilly station, Sudbury Town of 1931 (Fig 4.38), provided the template for many of the new

Fig 4.37
The sweeping, minimalist façade of Charles Holden's South Wimbledon, of 1926. (BB91/06861)

Fig 4.38
Sudbury Town of 1931. Transport for London still maintain Holden's original architectural details. (RO/24047/004)

underground stations that followed. Basically, it comprised a tall, rectangular brick box with a flat, concrete roof and large, vertical glazed strips running from the door lintels to the exaggerated frieze. Now listed Grade II*, Sudbury Town (which still retains many of its original fittings, including the 1931 ticket booths on both up and down sides) was described by Pevsner as 'an outstanding example of how satisfying such unpretentious buildings can be, purely through the use of careful details and good proportions.'[6]

At Arnos Grove (Fig 4.39), built in 1932 at the other end of the Piccadilly Line, Sudbury Town's rectangular box became a circular drum – a feature presumably inspired by the cylindrical rotunda of Gunnar Asplund's Public Library at Stockholm of 1928. Holden's most radical design, however, was for Southgate, of 1933 (Fig 4.40). Here the whole building is circular, with a glass clerestory – visibly supported only by a single column in the centre of the booking hall below – rising from the circular canopy. The clerestory was, in turn, topped by a tall, futuristic, illuminated finial – which, it has often been remarked, resembles an electricity-generating tesla coil, a potent symbol of the potential of electric power in the 1930s. Whilst

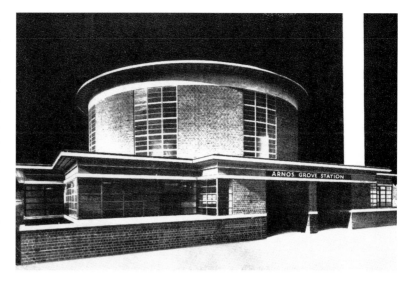

the station was partially modernised in 2008, it still retains its original escalator column lights, along with many of Holden's bronze panels.

Holden's last designs for London Transport were three new stations for the Central Line's eastern extension into Essex. Designed in the 1930s, their completion was delayed by the Second World War, and they were not finished until 1947. The new extension also appropriated some former GER stations. Indeed, in 1956

Fig 4.39 (above)
The wondrous drum of
Holden's Arnos Grove.
(RO/19118/001)

Fig 4.40 (below)
A beacon in the night:
Holden's futuristic
Southgate of 1933.
(RO/05715/004)

the brick, Dutch-gabled former GER station at Newbury Park of 1903 was actually demolished to enable widening of the adjacent A12, though its twin at Chigwell, further up the line, survives today.

Post-war austerity inevitably meant that the new above-ground buildings for the Central Line were far more ascetic and understated than Holden's pre-war stations. At Gants Hill (Fig 4.41), Holden was at least able to introduce an impressively majestic barrel vault, inspired by the Moscow Metro, into the platform-level concourse. But the most notable architectural feature of the Central's new 'Hainault Loop' was not Holden's restrained stations but the semi-circular, concrete-and-copper bus station by Oliver Hill built above Newbury Park Station in 1949.

Fig 4.41
Gants Hill's austere, Moscow-style interior of 1947. Holden had advised the City of Moscow on their Metro stations before the war.
(RO/22207/005)

5

Cathedrals of steam

The High Victorian era was an age of industrial and political confidence. And nothing exemplified this more than the increasing size and daring of England's principal railway stations – and the vaulting ambition of the railways that built them. Communities were razed, old and even relatively recent buildings were demolished, and churches and churchyards were ransacked and resited to make way for the new cathedrals of steam.

London

Charing Cross and Cannon Street

In London, all previous prohibitions designed to safeguard the sanctity of the City of Westminster were discarded in the name of technological progress. Thus the South Eastern Railway (SER) was finally allowed to cross the Thames after 1860, building impressive new termini on the river's north bank at Charing Cross and Cannon Street. At the former, Charles Fowler's Hungerford Market – a fine building not even 30 years old – was demolished in 1862 to make way for the new station, whose lofty trainshed was designed by Sir John Hawkshaw (1811–91) of the Great Eastern Railway (GER). The surrounding houses were all swept away, too: in 1861, one critic, evaluating the new Central London termini proposed by the SER and the Midland, claimed that 30,000 working-class inhabitants were dislodged to make way for the station. When finished in 1864, Hawkshaw's vast, single-span roof, sited at rooftop height at the end of his new, nine-span Hungerford Railway Bridge (which replaced the Brunel suspension bridge built as recently as 1845), towered over its surrounding neighbourhood. Disappointingly, though, the public face of the station, E M Barry's Charing Cross Hotel on the Strand (*see* Fig 1.18), completed in

1865, was decidedly less majestic. Repetitive and monotonous, the only real architectural relief was provided by its roofscape of dormers, chimneystacks, mansard-roofed pavilions and undersized pinnacles – all of which were removed in the post-war rebuilding programme of 1951.

In the event, both Hawkshaw's confidence and the SER's swaggering self-assurance were gravely misplaced. In 1905 Hawkshaw's great trainshed partially collapsed, killing six people. It was immediately replaced by a utilitarian post-and-girder structure, supporting a ridge-and-furrow glazed roof, which was in turn discarded when a new retail and office complex, designed by Terry Farrell and Partners, was introduced on the site in 1990.[1] Although the new Charing Cross complex's lowest floor reached right down to the level of the trains, at the summit of the development Farrell inserted two vast, elliptical arches, presumably intended to recall the span of Hawkshaw's doomed trainshed.

A mile east of Charing Cross, a vast area of Thames-side wharves and lanes was similarly demolished to make way for Barry and Hawkshaw's huge new Cannon Street Station. Hawkshaw's trainshed was twice the size of the Great Northern's at King's Cross, and its lofty, Wrennian towers sited at the southern end of the shed dominated the Thames waterfront. The Barry in this case was not Charing Cross's Edward Middleton Barry (1830–80) but the latter's younger brother, John Wolfe Barry (1836–1918). E M Barry himself later added the station hotel to the north in 1867. This design was a little more successful than that at Charing Cross, being saved from mundanity by two projecting turrets crowned with spires. However, this did not save the building from the post-war development. The single-span trainshed (Fig 5.1), which was still relatively intact, despite serious bomb damage in the war, was demolished in 1958, and Barry's hotel followed in 1960. In their place was erected an office block of breathtaking banality, built by developers Town and Country Properties and designed by their architect, John Poulson (1910–93). Poulson had won the Cannon Street contract (and that for work at Waterloo Station and the rebuilding of East Croydon Station, too) thanks to his wartime friendship with, and his subsequent – disarmingly paltry – bribe of £25 a week to a senior British Railways surveyor, Graham Tunbridge. At his trial in 1974, though, Poulson admitted that he had also given Tunbridge a cheque for only £200 and a suit worth £80 shortly before the Cannon Street contract was signed – hardly Las Vegas stakes. Poulson later served three years of a seven-year sentence – while Tunbridge was merely fined £4,000. And in 2007 planning permission was given to replace Poulson's dismal Cannon Street with a new and inevitably taller, mixed-use development by American developer Hines, which was designed by Foggo Associates. All that survives of the original 1860s station at Cannon Street are Hawkshaw's two soaring brick towers on the river front. These towers were listed in 1972, and in 1986 were restored by the Railway Heritage Trust – their weather-vanes being gilded to complement the dome of nearby St Paul's Cathedral.

Victoria and Broad Street

Upriver, the new terminus built at Victoria was promoted not by the railways themselves but, American-style, by a 'terminus company': the Victoria Station and Pimlico Railway. The first railway to use the site was the London, Brighton and South Coast Railway (LBSCR) in 1860, with a trainshed designed by John Fowler; two years later the London, Chatham and Dover Railway (LCDR) opened its own station on the southern half of the site. Victoria was no American union station, however: there was no communication at all between the two halves until 1924. The old, inadequate LBSCR head-building was replaced in 1908 by a new design by Charles Morgan – 'a large pompous Edwardian-baroque frontage'[2] in Biddle's opinion – whose upper floors merged into those of the adjacent Grosvenor Hotel, a ponderous, cliff-like building by J T Knowles of 1860–2 which popularised the French pavilion roofs later used at Slough Station and elsewhere. The southern, LCDR side

Fig 5.1
Cannon Street: the remnants of the trainshed pictured in c 1960.
(AA101191)

Fig 5.2
Arthur Blomfield's rebuilt terminus for the LCDR of 1909–10 at London Victoria.
(DD000447 [PDB01/01])

Fig 5.3
London's Broad Street Station in the last years of its existence.
(DD001509 [PDB01/01])

at Victoria – that had originally been provided only with a wooden-fronted building by the perennially impecunious railway (which had been dragged into bankruptcy by the Overend Gurney banking crash of 1866) – was rebuilt by its leaseholders between 1909 and 1910 to a design by Arthur Blomfield (Fig 5.2). The latter's new, stuffily neo-baroque stone façade, though oddly asymmetrical, did succeed rather better than that of its neighbour.

A mile away, in the City of London, the North London Railway – despite its relatively meagre network of lines – rejected the parsimonious meanness of Victoria's squabbling twins and decided to splash out on an exuberant terminus that could stand comparison with the best in continental Europe, let alone London. The exuberantly Franco-Italian (and, as it turned out, somewhat oversized) terminus at Broad Street (Fig 5.3), completed in 1865 to a design by William Baker, was an impressive essay in recession and mass entirely appropriate to a densely grained urban location. Its high French pavilion roofs with elaborate ironwork looked simultaneously grand and witty; and, in contrast to the cheeseparing at Victoria, a high quality of materials and design was used throughout the building – Venetian Gothic even being employed for the steep eastern stair to the high-level platforms. A century later, however, the station looked forlorn and run-down. Shorn of most of its routes, it was handling only 6,000 passengers a week by the early 1980s. In 1963 Beeching had recommended that it be closed, and although it was reprieved, in 1967 much of its trainshed was removed and in 1969 four of its nine platforms closed. Finally, in 1985, construction began on Rosehaugh's vast Broadgate development, whose bland new blocks would soon obliterate the station. On 27 June 1986, the last train for Watford Junction left the forlorn single platform that was all that was left of Broad Street. Weeks later, even this had disappeared.

St Pancras

The 1960s were difficult times for London's other northerly termini, too. The Hardwicks' Euston, as we will see (*see* Chapter 6), succumbed to the wrecking ball 20 years before Baker's Broad Street. St Pancras, however, after surviving numerous attempts to close and demolish it, fared rather better. Indeed, the successful campaign to retain and restore this magnificent station became a landmark in international conservation history.

Having shared King's Cross with the Great Northern Railway (GNR) for years – during which time the GNR made it clear that its junior partner was only there on sufferance, and repeatedly kept its trains waiting outside the station – the Midland Railway's plans for its own London terminus were ambitious and grandiose. The company decided to bridge its line over the Regent's Canal to the north, and not (as the GNR had done) to tunnel under it. As a result, despite the steep gradient trains had to negotiate into the new station, the trainshed and hotel at St Pancras were still built 6m (20ft) above the ground. St Pancras accordingly towered over its GNR neighbour, a result with which the Midland's directors were delighted. (The feud never really ended: even the two termini's clocks never told the same time.) To reach the station site, however, first the large and densely packed cemetery of Old St Pancras had to be levelled. The casual way this was first attempted, with coffins left lying open and human bones strewn about, caused great public offence after it was exposed by the newspapers. The architect charged with the reverent reburial, Arthur Blomfield (again),

employed as his assistant one Thomas Hardy, whose 1882 poem 'The Levelled Churchyard' imagined the churchyard's occupants' ...

sighs and piteous groans,
Half stifled in this jumbled patch
Of wrenched memorial stones!
We late-lamented, resting here,
Are mixed to human jam,
And each to each exclaims in fear,
'I know not which I am!'[3]

Inevitably, the trainshed (Fig 5.4) was the first element of St Pancras to be built, in 1865–8. At 74m (243ft) wide, it boasted the largest man-made span in the world for over 20 years (until Dutert's Palais des Machines in Paris of 1889). It was designed by William Henry Barlow (1812–1902), the Midland Railway's chief engineer, assisted by Rowland Mason Ordish (1824–86), an expert on iron construction who had worked at the Crystal Palace, Holborn Viaduct and the Royal Albert Hall. The shed's novel pointed shape was designed to give its inhabitants protection against the wind – though George Gilbert Scott, architect of the adjoining hotel, later mischievously declared that its profile was devised in anticipation of the style of his later building. And what appeared to be the concourse floor was actually a massive tie for the roof ribs, suspended above the real floor: Barlow intended the floor girders reaching across the station floor to form a ready-made tie sufficient for an arched roof crossing the station in one span. Below, cast-iron columns and brick piers under the concourse floor were spaced to accommodate barrels of Bass beer from Burton, delivered at the platforms' northern ends so as not to get the freight mixed up with the passengers. To the sides, the traditional distinction between masonry wall and iron-and-glass ceiling was dispensed with. Above, the shed roof incorporated two acres of glazing, while its massive iron ribs were pierced with quatrefoils, circles and stars. The ribs, which were originally coloured brown, were in 1876 repainted sky blue – a shade to which they have now returned. As the station's biographer, Simon Bradley, has noted:

Much of the visual power of this huge interior comes from the way in which these soaring arches allow the eye to calibrate the space immediately. Here are none of the distracting webs of sub-arches, braces and rods required by the sickle-truss roof, which tend to coalesce into a kind of visual mist in longer views (Scott called the system 'spider-like').[4]

In the year the great trainshed was begun, the competition to design St Pancras's hotel and offices of 1865 was won by the internationally celebrated George Gilbert Scott (1811–78), even though his scheme cost £50,000 more than the next cheapest submission. (Eventually two floors of offices and one floor of the hotel were omitted to trim the costs.) The choice of Gothic for such a large and visible public building (Fig 5.5) was inevitably controversial – coming only five years after Scott's Gothic design

for the Foreign Office had been rejected by the government. Architectural critic J T Emmett censured Scott's employment of 'ecclesiastical' Gothic, for 'catering for the low enjoyments of the great travelling crowd' and producing 'a complete travesty of noble associations' which Scott had 'not the slightest care to save ... from sordid contact'. Emmett recoiled with horror when he found that 'An elaboration that might be suitable for a chapter-house of a Cathedral choir' had been applied to the building, 'as an

Fig 5.4
Barlow and Ordish's
trainshed at St Pancras,
pictured c 1965.
(AA062189)

Fig 5.5
St Pancras's roofline c 1965.
(AA062320)

advertising medium for bagmen's bedrooms and the costly discomforts of a terminus hotel'.[5] More pragmatically, the architectural historian James Fergusson – who rarely had a good word to say about any contemporary buildings – thought, somewhat illogically, that both the hotel and the trainshed were actually too big, making the carriages and engines look like toy trains.

Yet, despite Emmett's charges, the station hotel at St Pancras was no medieval fantasy. Scott's iron girders were not hidden under plaster or masonry but, like those in the trainshed, were moulded and pierced to provide decor-

ation that, in good Ruskinian fashion, also served a sound structural purpose. His clock tower, too, was designed to be practical first, and romantically picturesque second. (Scott was the first to transfer this country house feature to the railway station.) Scott was also aware of the promotional imperatives behind the Midland's costly and ambitious enterprise. Accordingly, nearly all of his building materials were sourced from the Midland Railway's own network. The Gripper patent bricks were brought from Nottinghamshire; the Ketton stone and terracotta were from Rutland; the graduated slates were from Leicestershire; the fossil marble used for the internal columns was from Derbyshire; the sandstone from Mansfield; the limestone from Ancaster in South Lincolnshire; and the ironwork was by Butterley of Derbyshire (until 1867 the Midland was based in Derby). The iron and brass fittings by F A Skidmore of Coventry and the Minton tiles from Stoke, employed in the floors and dados of the hotel's enticingly curved main corridor, were also sourced from the Midlands, even though their cities of origin lay, regrettably,

on the London and North Western Railway (LNWR) network.

The centrepiece of the hotel, which opened as the Midland Grand, was the Grand Staircase (Fig 5.6). Here, Scott lavished six granites – pink Shap, grey Shap, grey Aberdeen, pink Devon and two Cornish varieties – to complement his generous use of native marbles in the rest of the building. (Green Connemara marble alternated with red Devon on the main corridor, for example.) The superb Skidmore ironwork

Fig 5.6
The bottom of the Grand Staircase at the Midland Grand Hotel, pictured 30 years after the hotel's closure.
(AA062204)

was set against a vaguely Tudoresque decorative scheme of red and fawn – soon discoloured by the gas from the light fittings and repainted in a more resilient, red-based scheme between 1886 and 1889. The artist, T W Hay, was commissioned not only for the murals in the Coffee Lounge – which were destroyed by the London, Midland and Scottish Railway (LMS) in 1935 – but also to paint a grand mural on the staircase's first floor landing: *The Garden of Deduit – Romance à la Rose*. At the top of the stair were decorated spandrels depicting nine 'Virtues' (a Victorian adaptation of the seven virtues of Catholic tradition which included Liberality and Industry), dressed in neoclassical garb and painted by Benjamin Donaldson to designs by the gifted but scandal-wracked architect E W Godwin.

Scott's hotel and offices were not planned in isolation from Barlow and Ordish's trainshed, as Furneaux Jordan's later charge of architectural 'schizophrenia' implied. Barlow had already planned the routes by which passengers and cabs would arrive at, pass through and leave the station, and Scott ensured his building adhered to this rational footprint. Scott and Barlow also ensured that the materials used to frame the trainshed harmonised with those used in the subsequent hotel. However, it would be naïve to expect a greater degree of aesthetic synchronicity. As Simon Bradley has noted, by the 1860s the demands and complexity of large railway stations, and the degree of specialisation expected from architectural and engineering practices, meant that 'Scott and his office no more had the expertise to design a structure as novel and audacious as the St Pancras trainshed than Barlow could have come up with a luxurious hotel expressed in advanced and coherent Neo-Gothic'.[6]

When it opened in 1873, the Midland Grand was the most luxurious hotel in the world. It boasted a pneumatic postal system, gas chandeliers, revolutionary Armstrong hydraulic lifts and equally innovatory rubbish chutes. It soon offered the first Ladies' Smoking Room to be found anywhere in the world. And it was emphatically *not* priced for the middling sort: the 1879 rate for one night's bed and breakfast, of 14 shillings, was the highest in London. Somewhat belatedly, though, the Midland suddenly decided that it had, after all, spent too much. In the year that their world-beating hotel opened its doors, the railway's construction committee controversially and brusquely

sacked George Gilbert Scott, the greatest architect of the day, and appointed the firm of Gillows of Lancaster to take charge of the interiors instead. Artist-architect Frederick J Sang was, at Scott's recommendation, initially put in charge of the details of the decoration, but he lasted only a year, being discharged in January 1874. Scott's failure to have the celebrated stained-glass workshop of Clayton and Bell involved in the decorative scheme was his last involvement in the project. Gillows completed the rest of the hotel in a more restrained manner than originally advocated by both Scott and Sang. In the event, though, what began life as the best hotel in the world lasted only 60 years before, starved of money and motivation, the building was shut by the short-sighted and philistine LMS of Josiah Stamp.

North and south

Middlesbrough

While critics such as Fergusson and Emmett were sceptical of St Pancras's charms, many contemporary railway architects were wholly inspired by the new cathedral. William Peachey of the North Eastern Railway (NER) designed the large, new station at Middlesbrough of 1877 in a chunky, robust, ecclesiastical Gothic that paid equal homage both to George Gilbert Scott's Midland masterpiece and to the animated Romanesque style of Henry Hobson Richardson. Middlesbrough's capacious booking hall featured a hammerbeam roof, and its external cornice a bold, scalloped parapet. Sadly, though, the splendid overall iron-and-glass roof – designed in collaboration with the NER's engineer, a Mr Cudworth, and hymned by an enraptured Carroll Meeks as 'the Sainte-Chapelle of trainsheds'[7] – was seriously damaged by bombing in 1942 and, after 1945, was removed rather than repaired.

Liverpool and Nottingham

At Liverpool, too, Lime Street Station was rebuilt as the St Pancras of the North-West. The new trainshed of 1867 by William Baker (Robert Stephenson's successor as chief engineer of the LNWR after the latter's death in 1859) had an iron-trussed span of 66.8m (219ft), which in 1874 was joined by a twin of an additional 56.7m (186ft) in width. The two structures constituted the first trainshed in which iron had been used throughout – with no brick walls or wooden panels. A second, parallel trainshed was completed to the south in 1879, to the designs of E W Ives and the LNWR's new chief engineer, Francis Stevenson, while the Gothic hotel just to the north of Lime Street, begun in 1867 and completed in 1871, was designed by the nationally experienced architect Alfred Waterhouse (1830–1905). Liverpool-born Waterhouse was best known in the 1860s for his work at Strangeways Prison in Manchester, Reading Town Hall and Oxford and Cambridge Universities; his Girton College, Cambridge had opened in 1870. He was still constructing his masterly Manchester Town Hall when the Great North Western Hotel – this prolific architect's only foray into railway architecture – was begun. Surprisingly plain in the treatment of its lower storeys, its roofline compensated for this modesty with an impressive array of turrets, pinnacles, pavilion roofs and dormers. Equipped with no fewer than 37 WCs and 8 baths for its 200 rooms when it opened, Waterhouse's hotel soared upwards like a French chateau in a marvellous advertisement for the LNWR. Nevertheless, Sir Josiah Stamp's impassive LMS had no compunction in clos-

ing the hotel in 1933. After decades as offices, and on the brink of dereliction, the building was saved in 1994 by Liverpool John Moores University, which converted the building into student accommodation and reopened it with much fanfare in 1996.

As we have seen at Charing Cross, bigger did not, though, necessarily mean more successful. Thomas Hine's new London Road (later Low Level) Station at Nottingham of 1857, for the GNR, for example, was an incoherent jumble of Tudor diaperwork, Jacobean gables and Georgian fenestration. Although the last passenger train departed the station in 1944, the building still survives, complete with its stone porte cochère, as a fitness club.

Bath and Bournemouth

In marked contrast to the behemoths of London and Liverpool, when the Midland Railway arrived at Bath, the company discarded both the Gothic style and the monumentality of St Pancras and Lime Street. Instead, it chose a scale and idiom fitting for this elegant city of modest Georgian terraces. Bath Green Park (Fig 5.7), by J H Sanders, was opened in 1869 – initially as Queen Square Station. A century

Fig 5.7
J H Sanders's Bath Green Park, opened in 1869 for the Midland Railway. (RO/33210/001)

Fig 5.8
The trainshed as the
station: William Jacomb's
Bournemouth East of 1885.
(RO/017465/006)

later, it was judged by Gordon Biddle to be a building 'of quite outstanding merit'.[8] With its well-balanced, parapeted elevation (although the pedimented windows in the two large end bays are really placed too low down the flanking pilasters), it played a major part in reinforcing the classical ambience of Bath. The station was closed in 1966 and remained derelict until 1983, when it was converted into a café and shops. The former platforms and tracks, still sheltered by J S Crossley's trainshed, are now used for car parking and markets, and lead to the superstore whose construction financed the rescue.

A deliberately low street frontage was also contrived at Bournemouth's principal station, which opened as Bournemouth East in 1885. It was built to the designs of William Jacomb, engineer to the London and South Western Railway (LSWR), and the absence of an architect was clearly evident from the external elevations of a building which used the services and offices as mere supports for the trainshed (Fig 5.8). The elevation to the south, for example, has no fewer than 22 repetitive brick bays, punctuated only by pedimented pilasters. At Bournemouth, the trainshed is definitely the

centre of attention, covering the four tracks with 12 immense, cross-braced wrought-iron trusses supported on open foliage brackets.

Return to London

Liverpool Street

Engineering also dominated at London's Liverpool Street, designed by the GER's chief engineer, Edward Wilson. Betjeman once called Liverpool Street 'the most picturesque and interesting of the London termini',[9] though he may have changed his mind were he to see it today. Its principal Decorated Gothic elevations, constructed at right angles to, rather than facing, Bishopsgate (for example, on the axis of the trainshed), were clearly influenced by Scott's Midland Grand at St Pancras, although they lack any of Scott's sense of height and vigour. And with some of the platforms extending further south than others – which Wilson dealt with by simply turning a corner in his façade, creating an L-shaped station – and extra platforms added to the east by W N Ashbee between 1890 and 1894, the terminus became a byword

Fig 5.9
Edward Wilson's fine
trainshed at London's
Liverpool Street
terminus, opened in
1874 and photographed
two decades before the
comprehensive rebuilding
and rationalisation of the
mid-1980s.
(AA061581)

for muddle and confusion (Fig 5.9). By 1950, the station's clock tower had lost its original pyramidal roof, and suddenly looked stunted and dumpy, while its Gothic façades were largely hidden behind the accumulated baggage of the station approach. When the station was rebuilt between 1985 and 1992 as part of the Broadgate development, the platforms were all brought to the same stop line, and the western elements of Wilson's excellent trainshed reproduced to the east. Stripped, cleaned, rationalised and filled with white-coated steel, however, the interior has lost much of Betjeman's 'picturesque' visual interest. The Great Eastern Hotel, added to the south of the station as an afterthought – astonishingly, neither Wilson nor his employers seems to have thought of building a station hotel before Liverpool Street opened in 1874 – has, though, fared better. Designed by E M Barry and yet another sibling,

his older brother Charles Barry junior (1823–1900), and originally opened in 1884, what is now the Andaz Liverpool Street still retains the music-hall-cum-Louis-XV plaster decoration of Hamilton Hall (now a pub), one of its two original Masonic temples (the outrageous first-floor 'Greek' version by Brown and Barrow of 1912), and many of R W Edis's exuberant interiors of 1899–1901, phrased in both *ancien régime* and Elizabethan idioms.

Marylebone

Colonel Sir Robert William Edis (1839–1927) was a colourful character. A grammar school boy, he became an assistant to Anthony Salvin before branching out on his own. As his private practice developed, he became adept at turning his hand to scholarly Gothic, the Aesthetic Movement's 'Queen Anne' style, the

Fig 5.10
R W Edis's Hotel Great
Central at Marylebone,
opened in 1899.
(AA063000)

baroque Revival manner, or whatever else the client preferred. He also managed to write two household manuals, *Decoration and Furniture of Town Houses* of 1881 and *Healthy Furniture and Decoration* of 1884, which both proved popular successes; stood successfully at the first London County Council elections in 1889 as a Tory-backed 'moderate'; and was a keen participant in that unlikely reserve regiment, the Artists' Rifles – receiving a commission in 1868, becoming its commanding officer in 1883, and holding the regimental office of honorary colonel from 1909 until his death. His knighthood of 1919 was not for his architecture but for his military service, which had helped to mould the Artists' Rifles into a formidable fighting force by the time of the First World War.

Edis's greatest achievement as a railway architect was his Hotel Great Central at Marylebone (Fig 5.10). This was not erected within the station footprint, but was built separately from

William Braddock's unassuming terminus of 1899. As early as 1895, the Great Central (formerly the Manchester, Sheffield & Lincolnshire Railway – popularly the 'money sunk and lost') realised it had no money left for a great London station incorporating a hotel, and sold the hotel site to the south of the station to furniture tycoon Sir John Blundell Maples. Maples opened his hotel, on time, in 1899, the same year in which the Great Central arrived next door. A much grander building than Braddock's station, it loomed ominously over its shrinking neighbour, its competent Queen Anne façades enlivened by a large, berserkly baroque clock tower. Braddock was not an architect but the Great Central's chief engineer, and his brick-faced station (Fig 5.11), built in a cheap and cheerful 'Wrenaissance Revival' style, was later compared by Betjeman to 'a branch public library in a Manchester suburb'.[10] Planned as an eight-platform station, the cost of Maryle-

Fig 5.11
London Marylebone's
unassuming façade at the
nadir of its fortunes in the
mid-1960s.
(AA063048)

bone was far higher than expected, and nearly bankrupted the Great Central; in the event, only half of the intended platforms at Marylebone were built. When the 'Beeching Axe' reduced Marylebone to the status of a suburban terminus – the furthest its services reached after 1967 was Aylesbury in Buckinghamshire – it looked as if even Braddock's modest achievement was imperilled. Edis's hotel also suffered from the vagaries of railway history: by the 1930s the hotel appeared doomed, and it was closed in 1936, not long after the Midland Grand to the east had also shut its doors. Both hotels were closed for the same reason: the railway company (in Marylebone's case, the London and North Eastern Railway (LNER) rather than the LMS) could not be bothered to update its facilities. The Hotel Great Central was first converted into offices, then served as a convalescent home during the Second World War, was used as a military headquarters after

1946 and subsequently, and bizarrely, metamorphosed into the headquarters of British Railways – in which guise it was known by staff as 'the Kremlin'. Vacated by British Rail long before the privatisation of the railways, after 1986 it was restored by Japanese developers to become, once more, an opulent hotel, which reopened in 1993 and which is currently known as the Landmark London.

The Midlands

Leicester, Derby and Sheffield

Edis was not the only architect to harness the fashion for expressive neo-baroque to railway architecture. Charles Trubshaw's Leicester Station (briefly known as Leicester London Road), rebuilt for the Midland between 1892 and 1894, was fronted by a powerful and lengthy porte

Fig 5.12
Charles Trubshaw's Sheffield
Midland Station shortly
before its evisceration in the
1960s.
(RO/01981/011)

cochère in Queen Anne style. This was punctuated with four massive baroque arches – the southernmost two of which were provided with massive, broken pediments in true Hawksmoorian style – which comprised separate entrances for incoming and outgoing passengers, and surmounted by oversized urn-finials and (at its northern end) by a finely proportioned, stone baroque clock tower with a 'beehive' roof and an octagonal lantern, which was itself provided with its very own, smaller beehive roof. Charles Trubshaw (1841–1917) was an architect's son and a surveyor to Stafford County Council who originally worked for the LNWR but, in 1874, was lured to the Midland Railway. While Trubshaw's *fin-de-siècle* tour de force at Leicester is still with us, however, Derby's classically arcaded street elevation of 1894 – terminated by two high Palladian pavilions, each with its own corner turret and cupola – was demolished as recently as 1985. Fragments of Trubshaw's Sheffield Midland station, however, still stand (Fig 5.12). Here the entrance and exit were originally planned via huge, pedimented arches at either end of yet another colossal entrance screen, this time executed in stone and arcaded with giant broken pediments. Today, with much of the original interior of the station – save the splendid First Class refreshment rooms, now an award-winning pub – having been demolished in favour of open, glazed spaces, Trubshaw's vast screen resembles an isolated relic from ancient Rome.

As we have seen, the Edwardian era saw stylistic diversity become the ethos of the age.

However, the day of the behemoth terminus was, in Britain at least, over. Most of the larger railways companies were experiencing financial difficulties even before 1914. After 1918, exhausted by the demands of the First World War, the railways were too weak to derail the Railways Act of 1921, which on 1 January 1923 herded them all into four convenient, quasi-nationalised 'Groups', which were then saddled with the Herculean task of trying to create a modern, cost-efficient railway from a bewildering maze of unconnected lines, ageing stock and brittle track.

Rebuilding cathedrals

Birmingham

Birmingham Moor Street, built by the GWR between 1909 and 1914 (Fig 5.13), was typical of the new realism. It was handsome, but it was cheap. Built of red brick with terracotta facings and stone dressings, its pastiche-baroque style suggested it was not taking itself too seriously. To save money, warehouses were actually built under the station after 1911, constructed in the manner pioneered by the French engineer François Hennebique (who used vast, reinforced ferro-concrete members which served both as upright and horizontal supports). Today, the station appears much as it might have been in 1914; but this is largely the result of a comprehensive rebuild of 2002–10, prompted by the growth in traffic to Snow Hill and beyond

– which saw Moor Street's through service restored in 2005. The tatty 1980s entrance was demolished, and the station rebuilt in an early-20th century idiom to match the style of the existing fabric.

Manchester

Also begun in 1909 was William Dawes's long Commercial-baroque rebuilding of Manchester Victoria (Fig 5.14). Dawes's elevations were unremittingly dull – in 1973 Biddle noted

the station was 'notable more for its size than style'[11] – but its dull, economical pomposity was enlivened by its cheerful, art nouveau refreshment room, which had been afforded a stained glass dome and mosaic lettering. By 2009 the station was in a very poor condition, but in February 2010 Network Rail announced it would refurbish the station as an interchange for local and regional services throughout the North-West, aided by the building of a rail chord to link it with the city's other surviving terminus, Piccadilly.

Fig 5.13
Birmingham Moor Street in the 1960s. Long neglected, today this station has been excellently restored and rebuilt, and is in full use once more.
(RO/017330/004)

Fig 5.14
William Dawes's Manchester Victoria, begun in 1909.
(RO/004090/008)

Waterloo

The only other substantial rebuilding project attempted by Britain's railway companies during the lean Edwardian years was the reconstruction and enlargement of London's Waterloo Station. Even then, the LSWR's approach was perfunctory and penny-pinching. The new station was admittedly big and busy; but it was not architecturally pleasing or technically advanced in the manner of American contemporaries such as New York's Penn and Grand Central Stations. (This was probably a major factor in the government's refusal to list the station in 2010.) The only real effort was expended on the new entrance to the northeast, built as a 'Victory Arch' between 1919 and 1922 by the LSWR's (soon the Southern's) in-house architect, J R Scott – and currently the only element of the site that enjoys the statutory protection of listing. Positioned at the summit of a flight of steps, with one side canted to fit into the existing station, Scott created a marvel-lously swaggering triumphal arch (Fig 5.15), which served both as a fitting last post for the 585 LSWR employees who lost their lives in the First World War (whose names are inscribed on brass plaques in the arch's soffit) and a last hurrah for the pre-Grouping independent railways. Dominating Scott's well-balanced composition are two sculptural groups by the little-known sculptor Charles Whiffen, very much in the manner of Jules Coutan's work atop the pediment at Grand Central: one group, of 1914, was dedicated to Bellona, the Roman goddess of war, and the other, of 1918, to Peace. These sit around a glazed arch, set with a clock in a sunburst and surmounted by the figure of Britannia. Unusually, the LSWR staff themselves were, consulted on the arch's design. Queen Mary herself opened the new Waterloo, with its 21 platforms, 240 synchronised clocks and its own telephone exchange, in March 1922. Today it still remains one of the most emotive expressions of the nation's railway heritage.

Fig 5.15
J R Scott's LSWR war memorial-cum-station entrance: the impressive Victory Arch entrance at Waterloo of 1901–22. (AA062053)

6

Demolition and decay

The blinkered evisceration of Britain's unique built railway heritage did not begin with the notorious 'Beeching Axe' of the 1960s. Indeed, the post-war razing of station buildings, often attributed to Beeching and his successors at the British Railways Board, actually began in earnest some years before the publication of the Beeching Report in 1963. The onslaught on one of Britain's finest and most characteristic building types should thus not be wholly blamed on the hapless figure of Richard Beeching (Fig 6.1).

Before Beeching

Many stations, indeed, had barely made it through the Second World War. After 1945, too, a near-bankrupt and war-weary nation had other more pressing economic priorities than maintaining Victorian railway stations, and often little thought was given to the longer-term economic or planning effects of closure. Thus, Moseley Station in Birmingham, serving one of the second city's most thriving suburbs, and Coborn Road (*see* Fig 1.13), serving a rather less affluent but nevertheless burgeoning population in East London, were both closed (and quickly demolished) at the end of 1946. The

creation of the nationalised British Railways (BR) in 1948 appears to have been the signal for the widespread removal of platform canopies, overall roofs and other station structures across the country in order to minimise maintenance tasks for a railway which increasingly could not find, or even pay for, the necessary labour.

By the time Beeching's report had been printed, many of the more uneconomic railways and stations had already disappeared. To take at random just one spread of R J V Butt's impressively comprehensive *Directory of Railway Stations* of 1995 ('Sc' to 'Se'): while many of the stations Butt records were closed in the post-Beeching era – such as the former London and South Western Railway (LSWR) stations at Seaton and Seaton Junction in Devon (Fig 6.2) in 1966 and the North Eastern's Seaton Delaval in 1964 – the majority were actually closed *before* Beeching's appointment. Scremerston and Seahouses – of the former London and North Eastern Railway (LNER) – closed in 1951; whilst 1952 saw the disappearance of the old North Eastern stations of Seaton

Fig 6.2
Seaton Junction, Devon.
(RO/08151/008)

(Northumberland) and Sedgefield, of the Great Eastern Railway's (GER) Sedgeford, and of Merseyside's Sefton and Maghull; in 1953 the old Great Northern Railway (GNR) station at Seacroft went; in 1954 the old North Eastern station at Scruton and Sedgebrook – of the London and North Western Railway (LNWR) – were axed; in 1955 the London, Brighton and South Coast Railway's (LBSCR) tiny station at Selham, West Sussex – largely surrounded by open fields – finally succumbed; in 1956 the GNR's Sedgebrook and the Liverpool Overhead Railway's Seaforth Sands shut; and 1960 the Wirral Railway's Seacombe and the LNWR's Sefton Park were both closed. And this over just two pages of the *Directory*.

By the time of BR's Modernisation Plan of 1955, BR had already realised that some of their operations could no longer continue, and were envisaging the closure of lossmaking branches and stations eight years before Beeching. By 1958, BR was addressing the issue with gusto, and the rate of closures doubled. Thus the East Grinstead to Lewes line perished as early as 1955, while almost the whole of the former Midland and GNR network, from Peterborough and Saxby to Norwich and Yarmouth, was closed in 1959.

In 1962 the focus moved from East Anglia to the South-West, as former Great Western Railway (GWR) branches found themselves subject to swingeing cuts. In that year the lines to Chard in Somerset were unceremoniously closed, though the Brunel-style Italianate brick buildings of Chard Central of 1866 survive today – sadly, the splendid wooden overall roof was swiftly removed soon after 1962 – as do the Brunel-inspired 'chalet' stations at Ilminster and Hatch, now a retail outlet and offices respectively. Also shut by BR in 1962 was the GWR branch to Helston in Cornwall – the site of the fine stone station of 1887 at Helston itself, a low, single-storey building with a steeply pitched roof and soaring chimneystacks – now covered by a housing estate; the former GWR branch to Buildwas and Much Wenlock; the branch to Chipping Norton; and the lines from Wolverhampton Low level to Stourbridge, from Bewdley to Tenbury Wells, and from Cheltenham to Kingham.

Thus many of England's historic railway structures had disappeared by the time Beeching's report hit the bookstands. Indeed, of the stations earmarked for closure by Beeching in 1963, 234 stations had already shut.

Euston

Perhaps the most famous pre-Beeching station casualty of all was London's vast terminus at Euston, whose demolition began in the year in which Beeching took his seat at the head of BR. In 1959, BR – having just added two new booking offices to Euston's concourse, thus introducing London's first mechanised ticket machines into the capital's oldest terminus – asked the London County Council (LCC) for permission to demolish the whole station. Notwithstanding the Euston Arch's worldwide renown as perhaps the most potent symbol of Britain's Victorian industrial achievements, let alone its pioneering role in creating the railways, Euston had always been rather an unloved station. Little affection had, understandably, been lavished on the site, aside from P C Hardwick's Great Hall and his father's imposing Arch. Its trainshed was uninspiring, its hotel was pedestrian, and access to and from its entrance was cramped and confusing. As early as 1898, the LNWR had suggested building an entirely new station on the site, but all that was done was to add a new booking hall to the south of the Great Hall just prior to the outbreak of the Great War – an addition which itself was upgraded in 1933 in what critics of the time, following Betjeman's lead, termed 'jazz-modern'. After the enforced 'Grouping' of 1923, the new London, Midland and Scottish Railway (LMS) sought to rationalise its London termini in the manner of the union stations now increasingly common in the large American cities. Euston's traffic, it was proposed, would be merged with that of St Pancras, and both stations were to be demolished. In the 1930s, even Betjeman himself thought that only the Euston Arch should be saved, and that the rest of the station could go.

The precedent of America's vast new union stations exercised a fascination for the British Railway planners and architects throughout the 1930s, and gave rise to a number of largely unexecuted schemes for rebuilding and combining London's great termini. Sir Henry Tanner, recently the author of pompous, Franco-American Beaux Arts classical façades on London's rebuilt Regent Street, proposed rebuilding Paddington as a vast classical pile, with lengthy colonnades and French 'Second Empire' pavilions occupying much of its Praed Street elevation – a façade which was to be paired with a giant new hotel on adjacent Westbourne Terrace. Much of Brunel and Wyatt's station, and certainly all of Hardwick's hotel, would have been demolished to make way for this monstrosity. At about the same time, the architect Percy Thomas – recently President of the Royal Institute of British Architects, and author of the soaring, stripped-classical Swansea Guildhall of 1930–4 – was chosen by LMS Chairman Lord Stamp to design a building to replace both Euston and St Pancras.

Josiah Stamp was a London School of Economics-trained economist (his *British Incomes and Property* of 1916 had swiftly became a standard work on the subject), who in 1919 joined the explosives company originally set up in Britain by Swedish chemist Alfred Nobel. This, in turn, metamorphosed into Imperial Chemicals Industries (ICI) – coincidentally, the same firm which was to spawn Richard Beeching. Given that Stamp was a leading British expert on taxation, it was somewhat surprising when in 1926 he was appointed chairman of the troubled LMS. Stamp made an encouraging start in this new role, bringing William Stanier over from the GWR as the firm's new chief engineer in 1932 and continuing the LNWR's pre-1923 electrification programme in London and the North-West. Having been knighted in 1920, in 1938 Stamp was raised to a peerage by his friend Neville Chamberlain – who was, in 1940, to make Stamp his last Chancellor of the Exchequer. More disturbingly, Stamp was also a leading member of the pro-Nazi Anglo-German Fellowship, set up in 1935, and personally visited Nazi Germany in 1936 (when he met Hitler) and again in 1937.

Whilst he proved an efficient administrator, Stamp was no fan of the LMS's remarkably diverse and significant architectural heritage. He made no secret of his loathing of the original designs of both Euston and St Pancras, both of which he publicly denounced as 'useless' and 'obsolete'. In 1935 – as St Pancras's Midland Grand Hotel was ignominiously closed, and potential overnight customers whisked away from St Pancras's forecourt to the mundane hotel at nearby Euston – he unveiled Percy Thomas's new scheme for a new union station-cum-hotel to replace both historic termini. Thomas's principal elevation was certainly monumental; but it was also disappointingly dull and lifeless, and conveyed little sense of the architectural heritage of either railway. Nevertheless, Stamp steamed ahead and, on 12 July 1938, threw a switch in Hardwick's Shareholder's Meeting Room at Euston to remotely

begin the quarrying of the limestone needed to construct Thomas's giant new station.

The outbreak of the Second World War in September 1939 saved Euston from demolition for the time being.[1] Indeed, between 1951 and 1953, BR sensitively restored Hardwick's Great Hall, suggesting to some that they might prove better custodians of the nation's historic stations than their pre-nationalisation predecessors. However, BR's 1959 application to demolish dashed all hopes that Euston was now safe in the organisation's hands. The newly founded Victorian Society of 1958 was equivocal about the site: in 1952 its chairman, Nikolaus Pevsner, had called the Euston Arch 'the greatest monument to the passing Railway Age', but the new society was happy to let the Great Hall and other historic interiors go. As a result, the fight concentrated on the survival of the Arch – which, placed as it was well to the south of the station building, could have been easily incorporated into any new scheme. In 1960 the Conservative-controlled LCC acceded to BR's application; moreover, the latter now announced that, whilst demolition of the Euston Arch would cost only £12,000, its re-erection elsewhere would cost a massive £190,000 (a figure that appeared to have been plucked out of thin air) – a 'financial burden' that BR self-righteously declared it was not prepared to bear. In July 1961, the government's Minister of Transport, Ernest Marples (more of whom anon), declared that the Arch, too, was to go – along with the rest of the station.

The subsequent battle to save Euston not only galvanised the nation's fledgling conservation movement – in much the same way that the campaigns to save Pennsylvania and Grand Central stations did in New York – but also witnessed the first alliance between conservationists and practising architects. Even the uncompromising modernist architect Alison Smithson wrote in *The Architect's Journal* that the Arch was …

… the last great classical building in the English sequence with an architectural merit which would make it welcome in almost any setting. Second, it is an important common-place in Victorian London … Third, it is a splendid reminder of our country's leadership in the early Railway Age. WE CANNOT POSSIBLY LET IT BE DESTROYED.[2]

Nevertheless, Ernest Marples (Fig 6.3) and his boss, Prime Minister Macmillan, were adamant that the whole site should be razed – even after the Victorian Society found a firm

of Canadian contractors who offered to move the Arch, on rollers, to a new site for less than half of BR's spurious quote. Demolition of the Arch accordingly began on 6 November 1961 (Fig 6.4), with the rest of the station following during 1963. Impressively, BR's demolition contractor Frank Valori actually numbered the individual stones on his own initiative in case the government or the LCC were to express a last-minute change of heart. With astonishing spite, however, BR's management ensured that the masonry of the Arch was dispersed across different, undisclosed sites. Two of these secret destinations were later identified by archi-

tectural historian Dan Cruickshank as a West London garden rockery and the bottom of the River Lea.

The rest of Euston Station, including the fine Great Hall of 1849, passed relatively unlamented. With predictable crassness, the new, bland, granite-clad concourse designed by the in-house architectural team at London Midland Region (LMR) – led by R L Moorcroft – was inappropriately named 'The Great Hall'. The unnecessary annihilation of the Euston Arch, however, continues to resonate to this day. Proposals continue to surface which envisage recreating the Arch in roughly its original position. Indeed, two of the small, classical pavilions which originally flanked the Arch are still there, sympathetically converted into CAMRA award-winning beer and cider bars. Richards and Mackenzie compared the demolition of the Arch to 'tearing down Salisbury Cathedral or Windsor Castle', and it is an act of sheer stupidity and vandalism for which revenge and restitution is still being demanded.

Euston's demise was but the first gust of an enormous storm that was to sweep across the nation, irrevocably changing the face of every English county (and those of Scotland, Wales

and Northern Ireland, too) for ever. In the spring of 1961, at the same time as Transport Minister Ernest Marples was rejecting widespread calls to save the Euston Arch, he was also removing an unknown, 47-year-old senior manager at ICI from his job as technical director and parachuting him into a five-year secondment as the new head of what became, the following year, the British Railways Board.

Vested interests: Ernest Marples

Richard Beeching was not from the same wealthy, privileged background as premier Macmillan, or the majority of Macmillan's cabinet. The son of a journalist and schoolteacher from Kent, he had attended grammar school, not public school, and had won his degree from Imperial College, not Oxbridge. Interestingly, his patron, Ernest Marples, was also a product of the grammar school system – in Marples's case it was Stretford Grammar rather than Beeching's Maidstone Grammar – and was one of the very few state-educated members of Macmillan's cabinet of 1960–1.[3] Marples had risen meteorically since Macmillan assumed the premiership after Eden's resignation, being appointed Postmaster General in 1957 and Minister of Transport the following year. In both posts, Marples demonstrated an unfailing talent for self-publicity, launching initiatives such as the Premium Bond, the first parking meters, the M1 motorway, traffic wardens and the MOT test with all the panache and media attention he could muster. He also oversaw the detaching of the nationalised railway system from the all-embracing British Transport Commission (BTC) in 1962 – though, interestingly, he never made any effort to privatise the railways – and simultaneously appointed Beeching, an outsider with no experience in the railway industry, to run BR. In the wake of BRs much-heralded Modernisation Plan of 1955, BR's deficit spiralled from £15.6 million in 1956 to £42 million in 1960 – by which time, railway historian David Clough has calculated, BR was effectively insolvent. Beeching's stark brief was to reverse the railways' mounting losses and 'return it to profitability' by whatever means he chose, whether by cutting services, lines or stations, or indeed all three.

Ernest Marples had a pressing personal interest in scaling the railways down. His professional background was as a building contractor, and after 1948 he had made a fortune through his civil engineering firm of Marples, Ridgway and Partners, building ports, power stations – and roads. On becoming a junior minister in Churchill's new Conservative government in November 1951, Marples resigned as managing director of Marples Ridgway but continued to hold 80 per cent of the firm's shares. When made Minister of Transport by Macmillan, in October 1959, Marples undertook to sell his shareholding in the company, as he was now in clear breach of the House of Commons' rules on conflicts of interest. But he had not done so by January 1960, when the London *Evening Standard* reported that Marples Ridgway had won the tender to build the Hammersmith Flyover – and, ominously, that the Ministry of Transport's engineers had endorsed the rejection of a lower tender. Marples's reaction to this alarming news was to attempt to sell his personal shareholding to Reginald Ridgway, from whom he aimed to buy his shares back at a later date; when that was blocked by the Attorney General, he simply 'sold' his shares to his wife.

Marples thus had a very powerful vested interest in shrinking the railways, in order to leave the way clear for contractors such as himself to build more, highly lucrative trunk roads and motorways. Between 1966 and 1967, for example, Marples Ridgway was the principal contractor for the multi-million pound London extension of the M1 motorway. Already, he had in 1960 halted any further spending on BR's Modernisation Plan – which, admittedly, had not effected any increase in railway revenues despite the substantial investment that the government had made in the system since 1955.

Marples's obvious conflict of interest was not the government's only headache concerning its Minister of Transport. At the same time as Beeching's report was being published in 1963, Marples was tangentially involved in the Profumo Affair, a sex scandal that ultimately helped to bring about Macmillan's resignation later that year. Lord Denning, chairing the enquiry into the matter, told Macmillan that a rumour that Marples was in the habit of regularly using prostitutes appeared to be true; predictably, though, this finding was omitted from Denning's final report. Twelve years later, and only months after he had retired as an MP, Marples fled to Monaco to evade well-substantiated accusations of major tax fraud, slum rack-renting and failing to pay former employees. He never returned to Britain, and died in 1978 in his Beaujolais vineyard.

'Beeching's Axe'

Beeching was an amateur in the railway world, economically out of his depth and politically awkward. And the report for which he was responsible had been commissioned by a minister who foresaw the rich pickings that would accrue to him and his firm once the building of motorways had superseded the government's investment in railways. Britain's railways were thus disembowelled by a man who should not have been let near a railway, let alone the Ministry of Transport, whilst the plan he cynically put in motion was devised by a figure who had no knowledge of modern transport systems and who, crucially, failed to take into account any future urban development. As a result, investment took second place to cuts. Thus, while Japan was building the world's first high-speed line, Britain – which had led the world in developing railways 130 years before – was blithely ignoring the railway revolution that this exciting new innovation had presaged.

The balding, moon-faced Beeching was certainly well paid for his work, earning more in a year than the Prime Minister and over twice as much as any other head of a nationalised British industry. This unusually high level of remuneration, indeed, became a subject of much discussion when Beeching published his report, *The Reshaping of British Railways*, in March 1963, particularly in view of the high level of job losses that his recommendations would inevitably cause. Beeching's findings suggested that 25 per cent of BR's income came from just 34 principal stations – a mere 0.5 of the total. His recipe to put British Rail into profit was to close 5,000 miles of track and a third of all stations: roughly 2,400 sites. Investing in growth – in high-speed lines, new inter-city links or even a cross-Channel link – was ignored in favour of major cuts: one-third of the country's 6,700 railway stations were to be shut (all in all, 2,363 stations were listed for closure), along with around 5,000 miles of track, a third of a million goods wagons and, over the next three years, around 70,000 railway jobs (over 25,000 going in the first phase alone). Beeching, a physicist not an economist, failed to appreciate that many of the minor branch lines fed into, or were fed by, the profit-making main lines, nor that their income was effectively included in that of the major stations. His bald conclusion was that 5,900 miles of branch line cost £20 million to maintain, but earned barely a quarter of that back. Beeching's fundamental mistake was to underestimate the contribution that branch lines made to the economics of the main lines, and indeed the railway system as a whole. Freight was to be the main revenue-earner for the post-Beeching future; passenger services were to be its poor relation. Yet Professor D L Munby, an economist at Nuffield College, Oxford, later calculated that the financial assumptions on which the Beeching Report was based – that a non-freight line needed 17,000 passengers a week to make it fiscally viable – were fundamentally flawed, and that the true figure in 1963 was a third less.

In the event, Beeching's remedy failed to cure the patient: BR's net operating deficit rose from £37.7 million in 1959 to £78.2 million in 1968. And, as Labour peer Lord Stonham pointed out in the 1963 debates over the report, the government's net subsidy to road transport, which went securely unchallenged, remained 'four times the railway deficit'. To solve the problems, BR needed more vision and insight than Beeching, Marples and Macmillan could provide.

Dispiritingly, Harold Wilson's incoming Labour administration of 1964 did little to end the negative Beeching culture of slash-and-burn. That year, Michael Flanders and Donald Swann published their wistful musical lament for Beeching's casualties, 'Slow Train'.[4] In December 1964, as a belated sop to Flanders, Swann and the many taxpayers who were outraged at the severity of the cuts, Wilson's government did announce that Beeching himself was to return early to ICI, in June 1965. But this did not prevent BR's chairman from being awarded a barony – and from launching, in February 1965, the 'second stage' of his plan: *The Development of the Major Railway Trunk Routes*.

According to Beeching's new blueprint, only 3,000 miles of railway were to be deemed deserving of 'future development', development which was to be concentrated almost solely on the East and West Coast Main Lines and the former GWR route to South Wales. The emptying of most of the main line to South Wales of intermediate stations in order to speed up services was a feeble attempt to replicate the Japanese bullet-train concept at a fraction of the cost, a policy which only served to deprive much of Oxfordshire, Wiltshire and Gloucestershire of valuable rail links while failing to deliver a genuinely high-speed service. Some lines which did survive – such as the LSWR's route to the South-West and the GWR's 'Cotswold Line' – were largely singled, an appallingly short-sighted strategy which British Rail's successors are currently spending millions of pounds reversing. By 1965, incidentally, the term 'Railways' was felt to be unhelpfully outmoded, and the national carrier began trading as 'British Rail'.

In the event, the Wilson government merely accelerated the speed of closures, adding routes such as the potentially lucrative Oxford–Cambridge line. Beeching's successor as chairman of the British Railways Board, Sir Stanley Raymond, actually presided over just as many station closures during his two-and-half years in office as did Beeching himself.

Some of the nation's finest landmarks of the industrial age perished in the subsequent fire sale. Although there was the odd reprieve – such as for the Central Wales Line, actually saved in February 1964 after Marples's personal intervention: a General Election was looming, and the line passed through a number of marginal constituencies – England's stations continued to be closed at an alarming rate. When the Haltwhistle–Alston branch was closed in 1976, the spirit of Euston still prevailed, and BR lifted the track with far more application and determination than it had shown in running the line over the past 30 years. Thankfully, Britain's railway enthusiasts are remarkably persistent and dogged: seven years later the narrow-gauge South Tynedale Railway (STR) opened on part of the former branch at Alston. Haltwhistle itself is currently in the STR's sights.

The destructive momentum of Beeching's report was still evident as late as 1981, when BR proposed closing the Midland's magnificent Settle–Carlisle line in view of the 'prohibitively expensive' cost of renewing the viaducts and tunnels. This scenic line, with its unique series of imaginative and solidly built stone stations, was only saved after much public outcry and media attention. This coverage in turn generated a 500 per cent increase in passenger traffic during the 1980s – a dramatic improvement which showed what strategic investment and marketing could do for Britain's railways. Astonishingly, though, even in the face of this signal success, BR still persisted with its closure plan for the Settle–Carlisle line and, in 1988, actually appointed bankers to deal with

the forthcoming sale. At the last moment, however, the Thatcher government stepped in to safeguard the route. In 2004 Network Rail finally announced a £60m programme of improvements for the line, including the refurbishment of those former Midland stations which still remained in railway hands.

The shadow of Beeching's axe fell far beyond the stations on lines now earmarked for closure. BR's short-term drive for 'profitability' and obsession with reducing maintenance responsibilities also threatened countless historic stations on surviving lines. Beeching's BR avowed that these sites could be made to be more cost-effective (if far less appealing to customers) if it erased buildings and removed staff. Yet the effect of this policy was akin to that of the Dissolution of the Monasteries of the 1530s and 1540s. Significant urban and rural landmarks, which had played a key part in defining and shaping the life of countless thousands, were thoughtlessly flattened. Fortunately, many of them – like the abbeys and monasteries of Henry VIII's day – quickly found new uses, generally as residential conversions (self-contained rural stationmasters' houses were obviously well suited for this purpose), or for retail or office use. But those station buildings which did not immediately attract a potential buyer were brusquely demolished in the manner of the Euston Arch, discarded as worn-out relics of a Victorian past of which the get-rich-quick proponents of Brave New Britain did not wish to be reminded.

A continuing decline

The closure of both local railway line and local station was often a death knell for rural villages. As historians Jeffrey Richards and John Mackenzie have noted:

The station was the hub of village life – a centre of news, gossip and advice, the home of bookstall and telegraph office. Its disappearance has been followed in many cases by that of the village shop, the village post office, even the village pub – the slow, inexorable process of rural decay.[5]

Today it is often difficult to find where the stations of closed railway lines even stood. Brunelesque chalets disappeared altogether from former GWR stops that were axed – stations such as Brimscombe in Gloucestershire, Southam Road in Warwickshire and Aldermaston in Berkshire – and even from those that weren't, such as Theale in Berkshire. In Devon, the soaring, bargeboarded gables of Tiverton Station, of 1885 (Fig 6.5), had been a familiar and much-loved local landmark for 80 years; yet the station buildings were levelled soon after the line lost its passenger service in 1963. In Somerset, the rebuilt station at Portishead (Fig 6.6) was barely a decade old when it was closed and demolished in 1964. The eradication of Portishead was one of Beeching's more inexplicable decisions: the station was a confident new building of 1954 which had been relocated to a more central, town-centre site and was serving a busy port. At the time of writing, it is proposed to reopen this branch and build yet another station for the reviving town – hardly the most sustainable of urban histories.

Further east, the GWR's handsome classical station at Abingdon of 1856, with its segmental pediment, was obliterated, as was the eccentric Tudor fantasy that was Yeovil Town Station, built in 1861 (partly by Tite?), shut in 1965 and swiftly razed to make way for a car park. All that remains to remember the handsome,

Fig 6.5
Beeching casualty: Tiverton Station of 1885.
(RO/08127/003)

Fig 6.6
Brand-new Portishead Station, of 1954; closed just 10 years later, in 1964.
(RO/04954/002)

Tudoresque stone station at Clevedon of 1847 is a pair of upended railways points which serve as a forlorn memorial to the town's lost railway connection. Similarly, there is nothing to be seen today of the LNWR/Buckinghamshire Railway's handsome, twin-gabled, white-brick station at Buckingham, opened in 1850 and closed in 1964.

Many fine stations were demolished unnecessarily. In the picturesque Gloucestershire town of Tetbury, the Brunel-inspired stone station of 1889 (Fig 6.7) was demolished after 1964 to make way for, once again, a car park. In Norfolk, the fabulous Arts and Crafts extravaganza at Mundesley-on-Sea of 1898 (Fig 6.8), its half-timbered gabled pavilions connected by a graceful, balustrade wooden arcade and its steeply pitched roof punctuated by chunky chimneystacks and a slender clock tower with a cupola, was demolished following closure in 1964. A housing estate was later built on the site of this, one of the most grievous architectural losses on the railway network. Further down the coast, the large, five-bay brick building at

Fig 6.7
Tetbury Station photographed in 1955. (RO/05993/003 © R M Casserley)

Fig 6.8
Mundesley-on-Sea, Norfolk: another Beeching victim. (RO/07058/001; © Andrew Muckley)

Aldeburgh, Suffolk, built by the Eastern Counties Railway (ECR) in 1860 (Fig 6.9), was demolished after closure in 1966 – BR being unable to predict the substantial seasonal traffic the seaside town would later develop through its invaluable association with Benjamin Britten. No traces remain today, either, of the large 1862 terminus at Hunstanton, a seaside town whose fortunes had been made by the arrival of the railway. The imposing, pedimented, six-bay Georgian villa – a classic Palladian composition of five bays with a one-bay extension – built in 1903 by the Norfolk and Suffolk at Yarmouth South Town, and which lingered until 1970 – has also disappeared.

Further north, all traces of the impressive brick station at Mablethorpe in Lincolnshire of 1873 (Fig 6.10) – which also closed in 1970 – have vanished, save a short section of platform which survives in a municipal garden. Yet another casualty of the 1970 emptying of East Anglia was the five-bay station of 1847 at St Ives (Fig 6.11), which was finally demolished in 1980. In 2009, a concrete-floored guided

Fig 6.9
The fine station at
Aldeburgh, of 1860.
(RO/05835/001)

Fig 6.10
Long-vanished Mablethorpe
Station, Lincolnshire.
(RO/17160/001)

busway was built over the former GER Cambridge–St Ives branch, necessitating the partial demolition of the well-proportioned white brick station, also of 1847, at Histon. Only a fierce local campaign prevented the whole building from being swept away to build a car park: it has often been suggested that the huge cost of the busway far exceeded the funds that would have been needed to reopen the original branch line. Meanwhile, the long, low granite station of 1877 at the other St Ives, in Cornwall (Fig 6.12), was closed and demolished in 1971,

and replaced by a lone platform with a simple shelter on the site of the goods shed.

Those stations most threatened by Beeching's scorched earth policy were the great Victorian city termini. Now that Euston had gone, it seemed that any great station was at risk, no matter how inspiring or important its design nor how illustrious its architect. When *The Reshaping of British Railways* was published in 1963, and the wrecker's ball was laying waste to the Hardwicks' Euston, St Pancras was widely believed to be earmarked as the next

Fig 6.11
St Ives, Cambridgeshire: demolished in 1980. (RO/05057/003)

Fig 6.12
Needless demolition: St Ives Station, Cornwall, before evisceration. (RO/07834/004)

victim of BR's rationalisation. In 1939 even the heritage-conscious architect-critic Sir Albert Richardson had proposed demolishing Scott's Midland Grand Hotel to improve the view of Barlow and Ordish's trainshed behind. In 1966, with Euston successfully razed, BR announced plans to amalgamate King's Cross and St Pancras into a 'single modern terminal'. The site of St Pancras would instead be filled with a sports centre or exhibition hall, in spineless emulation of the dismal, anodyne Madison Square Garden complex then being built upon the ashes of New York's Penn Station.

This new threat to St Pancras incited the Victorian Society to swing into action. Its first secretary, John Betjeman, damned the proposed demolition as 'a criminal folly'; the society's chairman, Nikolaus Pevsner, daringly labelled the building 'a masterpiece of modern architecture'; while Victorian Society supporter, artist John Piper, hymned the site as 'a great Gothic phantasmagoria' whose 'value to the London skyline [was] inestimable … high as a cliff crowned with a pinnacled castle in a Grimm's fairy-story [with its] sky-assaulting rage of turrets'.[6] In the event, and to some surprise, the Labour government sided with the conservation lobbyists rather than with the vested interests. In November 1967, the station complex was awarded one of the first 'Grade I' building listings, enabling St Pancras to enjoy the protection of the tougher historic buildings legislation recently passed by Harold Wilson's government and to join a new, elite club of outstanding historic structures that included Westminster Abbey and Windsor Castle.

Regrettably, the famous victory won at St Pancras was rarely repeated elsewhere. Indeed, the list of fine stations needlessly sacrificed in the 1960s and 1970s to the goal of creating a low-maintenance railway system – and flattened before a new, alternative use could be found – is depressingly long. As we have seen, even those stations on lines which remained open after Beeching's report were not safe from destruction. All of BR's new regions were to some extent to blame; none more so, though, than Southern Region, which in the late 1960s embarked on a wholesale station demolition programme on those lines which remained. The large Gothic villa of 1902 at Christ's Hospital was replaced with a single-storey brick structure, the design of which would shame many a public toilet. The delightful gabled building at Dorking West (formerly known as Dorking Town, and already unstaffed from 1963), with its superb decorative bargeboards and fake timber framing, was destroyed; two decades later the handsome brick building of 1867 fronting Dorking's LBSCR station was also torn down, replaced by a block of appalling mediocrity. Southern's myopic management also razed the handsome brick building of 1910 at Blackwater, which boasted a vast, segmental pediment over its entrance; the splendid, pedimented, two-storey Italianate elevations of Paddock Wood of 1842; South Eastern Railway's fine, gabled Italianate composition at Gomshall and Shere of c 1850 (Fig 6.13), which had provided a delightful, odd contrast to its Gothic-vernacular neighbours on the North Downs line; and the fine, 'moderne' buildings of 1938 at Temple-

Fig 6.13
Gomshall and Shere.
(RO/06451/001)

combe, demolished soon after the station was closed in 1966. Thanks to pressure from local lobbyists, however, Templecombe station itself, without any of its original architecture, was finally reopened in 1983.

In South London, Forest Hill – opened in 1839 as 'Dartmouth Arms' (Fig 6.14) and renamed Forest Hill in 1845 – had been rebuilt in 1854 and again in 1881, this time by F Dale Banister, and was definitely something special. Its down building featured three large arches below a 'perpendicular' tower with a pointed

roof and two-bay wings; on the up side, a massive clock tower also served as a porte cochère – added, Biddle suggests, 'for the benefit of some of the top railway officials who lived in the district'.[7] Yet all of this fine architecture was demolished by Southern in the late 1960s, replaced by a mean and flimsy system-built structure (Fig 6.15).

Redundant stations in isolated rural contexts were, understandably, more likely to be converted for residential use than those in urban locations, few of which survived. Thus the

Fig 6.14
The original Dartmouth Arms Station at Forest Hill of 1839.
RO/22206/007

Fig 6.15
Forest Hill's dismal 1960s replacement.
(© 2010 Sunil060902, used under a Creative Commons Attribution-ShareAlike licence:
http://creativecommons.org/licences/by-sa/3.0/.
Taken from
http://en.wikipedia.org/wiki/Forest_Hill_railway_station)

*Fig 6.16
Burton-upon-Trent Station,
demolished in 1970.
(AA70/02617.
Reproduced by courtesy of
Staffordshire Record Office
[C/P/65/2/1/12/25/1])*

imposing brick towers at Wood Green's Palace Gates terminus of 1878, a station closed in 1963 (three months before Beeching's report was published), were demolished in 1968, though the track and platforms survived until the mid-1990s. At Burton-upon-Trent – a station actually not threatened by Beeching's cuts – the fine old Victorian station of 1875 (Fig 6.16) was demolished in 1970 and an apologetic brick structure, with only a blank lift tower for vertical emphasis, erected in its place in 1972. British Rail even suggested that J P Pritchett's magnificent Huddersfield Station be demolished – a philistine proposal which would have torn the

heart out of Huddersfield's historic centre. This horrific suggestion was, thankfully, quashed. Yet in 1970, and again in 1972, the same was suggested for one of the nation's most important and striking urban stations: John Dobson's marvellous Newcastle Central. All of Dobson's splendid work was to go, and the station was to be rebuilt behind Prosser's porte cochère. Mercifully, pressure from the Victorian Society convinced Newcastle City Council to reject this distressing proposal.

Whilst Newcastle saved its station, many great Victorian towns and cities connived with BR and with local developers to lose theirs. E A Cowper's splendid trainshed roof at Birmingham New Street (*see* Fig 1.11) had been badly damaged by bombing in 1940, and was later demolished rather than rebuilt; now, after 1964, the whole of Livock's station – including the Queens Hotel – followed. At Birmingham Snow Hill, J A Chatwin's Great Western Hotel of 1875 (Fig 6.17), which Andy Foster's new Pevsner guide calls 'the finest 19th century hotel in the city',[8] was demolished between 1969 and 1971, while Walter Armstrong's trainshed of 1906–11 (Fig 6.18) perished in 1976. In Birkenhead, R E Johnstone's Woodside Station of 1878, phrased in an attractive if rather incoherent red-brick 'Venetian Gothic' style and with a fine trainshed covered by two large, wooden

*Fig 6.17
Chatwin's Great Western
Hotel at Birmingham Snow
Hill.
(BB65/04344)*

spans was closed in 1967 and demolished to make way for a bus park. Luckily, the same town's Hamilton Square Station, built by G E Grayson for the Mersey Railway and opened in 1886, managed to survive, protected by listing. Today its tall, brick hydraulic tower remains a much-loved local landmark.

Top of the list of those urban stations earmarked for demolition after 1963 were the principal stops of that Johnny-come-lately of the great trunk routes, the Great Central Railway (GCR). Admittedly few of the cash-strapped GCR's stations were architectural gems, and all of the larger towns it served offered other station alternatives. Surprisingly, the brick frontage of Leicester Central of 1899 (Fig 6.19) still survives, although rather mutilated, as part of a commercial development; but

Rugby Central and Mansfield Central (Fig 6.20) were quickly demolished after closure. Perhaps the best of the GCR's new London Extension stations had been Nottingham Victoria, of 1900. Designed by local architect A E Lambert (who also rebuilt Nottingham Midland, now Nottingham's only main-line station), the station was devised as a riot of Jacobethan and baroque motifs: Dutch gable ends, pedimented gables, heavily rusticated columns, a wooden cupola and open, segmental pediments all competed joyously for attention. Yet after the station closed for business in September 1967, almost the whole site was flattened to make way for a shopping centre, in the midst of which Lambert's cheerfully eclectic clock tower now stands, wistfully marooned. Further north, while the former GCR station at Gainsborough

Central still exists, its loftily arched, three-bay porch of 1849 was inexplicably demolished in 1976.

Great stations were also lost on saved lines. J B Fraser's assertive station at Wakefield Westgate of 1867 (Fig 6.21), provided with one of the most eccentric clock towers in the country – a fusion of art nouveau and Gothic styles, 29.6m (97ft) high, and decorated with a cast-iron lantern and a gilded weathervane – was ruthlessly rationalised and downsized. All that survived of Fraser's work were pared-down brick structures on the up side, which now lost its valuable bay platforms. Ironically, Westgate's low-cost replacement – a mean, two-platform station with a small, low bridge and a grossly undersized, tiled booking hall, all of which was clearly unfit for purpose from the day it opened

Fig 6.20
Mansfield Central.
(RO/21827/001)

Fig 6.21
Wakefield Westgate c 1970.
(RO/06610/005)

– was itself demolished in 2013 and replaced by a new, larger, golden-clad bridge and glazed booking hall to the north, built on an extension of the existing platforms.

The charming 'half-timbered' buildings of Kidderminster of 1863 were senselessly demolished in the 1970s, as were Bedford Midland's wonderful, unique series of glazed iron canopies – which, when demolition began, fell onto one another like a line of glass dominoes. The red-brick Gothic station of the 1880s at Kenilworth went in 1965; only in 2008 was it belatedly realised that this thriving, growing Warwickshire town really should have retained its station, and funding was finally secured for its rebuilding in 2013. Also demolished in 1965 was William Peachey's excellent station at Sunderland of 1879 (Fig 6.22), with its St Pancras-style Gothic clock tower and grand, three-arched porte cochère. Sunderland was to experience many architectural and economic knocks over the next four decades, but the loss of Peachey's station was one of the most senseless and unnecessary blows.

The irrational demolition of the nation's railway heritage carried on well into the 1980s. In 1985 Derby's fine, Wrennian station building, with its imposing colonnaded entrance, was extinguished to make way for a mediocre brick structure, equipped with a feeble clerestory of dismally uninspired design. The station was at least rebuilt again, after 2001, in a more inspired and aspirational, high-tech style.

Down but not out

Today, reassuringly, many closed railway stations still remain in existence, albeit serving a very different function. The well-built stone station at Wadebridge, Cornwall, immortalised in verse by John Betjeman but closed in 1967, still survives (along with its platform canopy) as a day-care facility named, appropriately enough, the Betjeman Centre. Further up the line, Padstow Station of 1899 (Fig 6.23) now houses the local town council, although today the original building sits stranded in a sea of asphalt. The terminus of the LSWR-worked Sidmouth Railway, a splendid, two-gabled brick

Fig 6.22
Sunderland Station, shortly before the historic fabric at the rear was demolished. (RO/16092/002)

Fig 6.23
Padstow Station, photographed in 1926. (RO/07818/002 © H C Casserley)

building of 1874, is now offices. Further along the coast, much of Bridport Station in Dorset of 1857 has been relocated to the Beer Heights Light Railway, while nearby West Bay Station of 1884 remains in its original location, long bereft of its railway but operating as a successful café. The now-trendy Dorset town of West Bay has had a chequered history. The LSWR gave up on developing the small port as a resort as early as 1930, and it became a forgotten backwater. Rehabilitation and gentrification of the town only began in the 1990s, a process which was given a substantial shot in the arm in 2013 when the town was used as the primary location for the cult TV drama *Broadchurch*. All

of this newfound popularity suggests that the LSWR should have hung on.

In Norfolk, the handsome, three-bay Georgian domestic brick station at Wells-next-the-Sea of 1857 survives as a shop and pottery. William Bell's fine, rebuilt NER trainshed at Alnwick, Northumberland, of 1887, is now a hugely successful second-hand bookshop, passenger services having been shortsightedly withdrawn from this wealthy town in 1968. On the GWR's closed Didcot to Newbury line, Upton and Blewbury (Fig 6.24), Compton and Hermitage stations all survive as private homes, if substantially altered. The splendid Gothic pile at North Tawton of 1865 (Fig 6.25),

Fig 6.24
The GWR's Upton and Blewbury: opened in 1863, closed in 1962. The station building survives in residential use, reached by a road ironically named 'Beeching Close'.
(RO/07345/002)

Fig 6.25
North Tawton, Devon, shortly before closure.
(RO/06669/001)

Fig 6.26
Hornsea Town after
conversion.
(AA98/13618)

with its sets of triple arched windows, is also a private house, while the similarly designed Tavistock North of 1890 now offers self-catering accommodation. North Tawton was once at the centre of a network of LSWR main and branch lines, but in 1972 the last of its train services was removed. There is still the possibility that services may be reintroduced, however, as the Dartmoor Railway passes right by. Also currently under consideration for reopening is the GWR's former Torrington branch – closure of which to passengers in 1965 killed off much of the tourist trade in this picturesque part of North Devon. Fortunately, the branch's solid stone stations at Torrington and Bideford still remain relatively intact, in private hands.

The fine Jacobean station at Sandon, Staffordshire, of 1849–50, with its tall, Tudorist chimneystacks, porte cochère (provided for the use of the second Earl of Harrowby) and diaper brickwork, is also a private residence, as are the tiny stone stations at Avonwick, Loddiswell and Gara Bridge on the GWR's Kingsbridge branch in Devon, the first two of which still retain their single platform. All of the stations of 1853–4 on the Hull–Withernsea branch of the Hull and Holderness Railway (bought by the NER in 1862) survive in some form, mostly as homes – all except the Withernsea terminus itself. The same is true of the Hull and Holderness's former branch to Hornsea. Here the eastern terminus – the fine station at Hornsea Town by Rawlins Gould of 1850 (Fig 6.26), with its outstanding, five-bay porte cochère – has been converted into offices. Another excellent North-Eastern station, G T Andrews's splen-

did Richmond, built in 1847 for the GNER, is now an arts centre. The marvellous turn-of-the-century extravaganza at Bexhill West, as we have seen, remains in use as offices, a pub and a restaurant. And many of the Midland and Great Northern (M&GN) stations in Norfolk – brick-built structures, such as Corpusty and Saxthorpe of 1887 (Fig 6.27), notable for their elaborate bargeboards – are today private homes. Their survival may be due to the fact that, when most of the M&GN's Norfolk system was closed in 1959, the property market in East Anglia had not been flooded with rural railway stations. Thus, when the Maldon branch in Essex closed beyond Braintree in 1964, while the fabulous Jacobethan brick pile at Maldon East and Heybridge found a new use, most of the half-timbered stations on the way to Maldon subsequently perished – redundant railway stations being suddenly very commonplace in this part of the world.

Fig 6.27
Corpusty and Saxthorpe:
a typical Norfolk country
station, closed in 1959.
It survives, alone with its
platform, as a private home.
(RO/06881/001)

Not every closed urban station was immediately felled, either. The GWR's Wolverhampton Low Level of 1853–4 (Fig 6.28) is a happy exception to the rule. Originally built by John Fowler for the Worcester, Oxford and Wolverhampton Railway, the Birmingham, Wolverhampton and Dudley Railway and the Shrewsbury and Birmingham Railway, it boasted a handsome, Palladian-style, five-bay villa frontage, complete with a pediment over the projecting central three bays, and a full-height booking hall with paired Doric and Ionic pilasters. It lost its Brunel-designed ridge-and-furrow overall iron roof back in 1922, when the original covering was replaced by platform verandahs on cast-iron columns. It was closed to passengers in 1972, to freight in 1981 and to BR's engineers in 1986. After a variety of reuse options failed, including as a museum and a conference centre, it lost its rail connection in 2005. Protected by its Grade II* listing, however, the former station was subsequently incorporated into a new office and leisure development in what was now branded as the 'Canalside Quarter'. In a similar vein, as we have seen, J H Sanders's handsome, classical head-building at Bath Green Park Railway of 1869 prospers today as the frontage to a superstore of 1983, hosting a café and shops, while its 14-bay trainshed by J S Crossley now shelters a farmers' market as well as a car park.

Some Victorian stations survive as hotel accommodation. The handsome if remote station at Petworth of 1867 (see Fig 3.4), with its neo-Georgian sash windows, its weatherboarded walls and its projecting, five-bay front, is now an upmarket bed-and-breakfast hotel, with breakfasts being provided in the station and accommodation in former Pullman carriages parked in the sidings to the east. While Petworth Station's isolated location and ultimate demise was the result of the local aristocrat's refusal to allow the railway to proceed across his land, the station at Alton in Staffordshire, opened on 13 July 1849, was designed in a sturdy Italianate style to serve specifically as the stop for the Earl of Shrewsbury's vast, adjacent stately home at Alton Towers (Fig 6.29). Lord Shrewsbury even had a luggage lift installed at the station to hoist his baggage up to his home, which was atop nearby Bunbury Hill. The station itself comprised a delightful, chalet-like main building, housing the booking hall and waiting room, set alongside a three-storey tower-house which contained the stationmaster's house and, on the ground floor, the Earl's suite of waiting rooms. Renamed Alton Towers in 1954, the station closed ten years later – only to be reopened as prestigious and atmospheric holiday accommodation by the Landmark Trust in 1972. The fact that both the listed station buildings, the two platforms and the trackbed are in good condition has, in view of the vast commercial success of Alton Towers as a visitor attraction, encouraged one company to seek to reopen the railway link to Alton Towers Station, restoring the train service from Stoke and Leek lost in 1964.

Other stations have, in the American model, been converted as restaurants or bars. Following a devastating fire of 1980, the impressive

Fig 6.29
Alton Towers.
(RO/04201/001)

Italianate façade of the LBSCR's Denmark Hill of 1864–6 now fronts a celebrated and successful pub. The splendidly imposing Victorian brick-and-stone confection of 1866 at Tunbridge Wells West (Fig 6.30), probably designed by the LBSCR's chief engineer, F Dale Banister, has a long, two-storey platform façade, bookended by two gabled pavilions, and a confident clock tower, topped with a pyramidal roof and lantern. It is now a Wild West-themed restaurant. The station – justifiably called the 'St Pancras of the Weald' by locals – closed as recently as 1985, at which time its evocative panelled booking hall was still gas-lit. Listed the following year, this fine example of High Victorian taste and ambition prospers in restaurant use, albeit that the building and its one adjacent platform are marooned in the midst of a supermarket car park. Whilst the privately run Spa Valley Railway to Eridge, opened in 1996 on the recently closed LBSCR route, now runs from a modern platform to the west of the car park, Sainsbury's has agreed to maintain a corridor to enable any reinstated line to run through to Banister's exuberant terminus at a future date.

Fig 6.30
Tunbridge Wells West of 1866.
(RO/06988/001)

After 1963, even those branch lines which retained their services, and which were in good economic health, found their Victorian or Edwardian stations demolished and replaced simply with a functional platform or two. The three decades which followed the Beeching Report also saw the growth of the lamentable policy of selling town-centre station sites for their development value, and building a minimalist new terminus – often just a single, empty platform, occasionally furnished with a perfunctory bus shelter – a few hundred yards down the line. As noted above, the fine terminus of 1877 at St Ives in Cornwall, sited on a sharp curve, was demolished in 1971, and a single replacement platform built a few hundred yards to the south. The site of the old station is now merely a car park. The single-storey Tudor station at Henley-on-Thames was demolished as late as 1975, with a utilitarian substitute completed on roughly the same site only a decade later. Its branch line station buildings were demol-

ished as late as 1985, and replaced by flimsy shelters. At Cromer in Norfolk, BR withdrew from the fine, half-timbered building – which thankfully survives as a pub – in the 1990s and built a new island platform down the line, equipped with only a tiny shelter.

Sadly, the age of station demolition is not over. Uckfield's characterful country station and Hastings' fine art deco landmark were, as we have seen, razed in 2000 and 2004 respectively. And as late as 2009, the delightful, stone-built but strangely unlisted GWR station at Bourton-on-the-Water (Fig 6.31) was flattened, having been branded an 'eyesore' by a local councillor and razed to make way for a care home. It had been hoped that the nearby Gloucestershire Warwickshire Railway would rebuild the building at Broadway; in the event it was able to extend its line from Toddington, but funding was not available and, without the protection of listing, the station disappeared. The threat to our precious railway heritage has, clearly, not evaporated.

Fig 6.31
The GWR's Bourton-on-the-Water Station: demolished only in 2009.
(© David Mytton)

Brave new British Rail

Thirty years ago, social historians Richards and Mackenzie noted that, 'In an age which can design its high-speed trains to resemble aeroplanes and its low-speed trains to resemble buses', it was hardly surprising that 'its stations should equally have no identifiable association with the railways'. 'The symbol of the new age', they concluded, 'is the new Euston, an all-purpose combination of airport lounge and all-purpose public lavatory'.[1]

Certainly much of the new station architecture of the post-Beeching era appeared to tally with this thesis. Its rationale was underlined by the depressing comments made in 1976 – both by British Rail's outgoing chairman, Sir Richard Marsh, that 'There is nothing romantic about the railways', and by his incoming replacement, Peter Parker, who complained that the drive to modernise existing stations was hampered by the number of listed stations that British Rail owned. The truth was that, by the time Marsh had slunk off the national stage, many of those railway stations which had managed to outlast the post-war cull had seen their historic structures mutilated or annihilated. At the same time, the exciting new railway architecture that had been developed in the late 1950s and early 1960s had, by the end of the 1970s, descended into bland, weary mediocrity.

Modernisation

The age of 'Never Had It So Good' had started out with such high hopes. The electrification of the West Coast main line, recommended by the Modernisation Plan of 1955 and begun four years later, involved the rebuilding of many of the line's stations. And most of these were invariably remodelled in the new, internationalist modernist style, with varying degrees of success and individuality.

The first of these brave new stations was at Potters Bar in Hertfordshire, where the station was wholly rebuilt by British Railway's (BR) Eastern Region (project architect J Wyatt) in 1955 (Fig 7.1). A delicate, well-proportioned glazed entrance with a high clerestory led to platforms covered by innovative awnings of pre-stressed concrete. The result was handsome, neat and airy – a splendid start for the Modernisation Plan. Nikolaus Pevsner later eulogised the design as 'The first of the Eastern Region's good modern stations',[2] and it seemed to provide an excellent template for the future.

Fig 7.1
Potters Bar: the first station completed following the publication of British Railways' Modernisation Plan, in 1955.
(RO/24186/004)

Some of the London Midland Region's (LMR) new stations, too, were markedly successful. The region's chief architect, W R Headley, oversaw the creation of a number of strikingly new and daring buildings – although many historic structures were inevitably sacrificed to provide *Lebensraum* for these confident and promising new constructions. Slab roofs atop modernist modular structures were introduced at many smaller new stations such as Heald Green and Burnage, of 1959, and Hartford and Styal, both of 1960. At Coventry Station (Fig 7.2), which opened in 1962 on a site which had been shattered by bombing between 1940 and 1941, Headley and project architect Derrick Shorten created an imaginative new template for the larger station: a spacious, concrete-framed, glazed booking hall with a cantilevered roof, and of two storeys (still, at time of writing, mercifully free of the Lilliputian litter of automated ticket barriers), with its high ceiling finished in varnished hardwood strip boarding. The fact that this shiny new station dismally failed to relate to the architecture of the new city centre, and was soon to be confined within the hellish girdle that was the city's inner ring road, was not the fault of the architects but of the city council. Coventry Station had, by the time the building was publicly unveiled on 1 May 1962, been interpreted by many observers as a harbinger of the city's rebirth – almost as powerful a symbol of the new city as Basil Spence's new Coventry Cathedral, which opened later the same month.

While Coventry Station was impressive, LMR's station at Manchester Oxford Road of 1960 (Fig 7.3) remains Headley's masterpiece. Working with project architect Max Glendinning, Headley created a dramatic structure of prow-like, laminated timber shells of increasing size, which stretched across the entrance and booking hall in the manner of Jørn Utzon's recently begun Sydney Opera House – a comparison which was, and is, well-deserved. Over the platforms the shells – made of timber, rather than concrete, so as to reduce weight – became big, curved wooden canopies. This outstanding, listed structure is, at the time of writing, due to be remodelled to enable more traffic to pass through the site; it is to be hoped that Headley and Glendinning's fine, compact architecture survives the process unscathed.

Western Region's Banbury (Fig 7.4) (then called Banbury General) was another beneficiary of BR's ambitious Modernisation Plan. Rebuilt generously in a modernist idiom between 1958 and 1959, it was provided with bay platforms, lift towers and a fine, glazed principal (western) elevation. Critics of the railway were quick to seize on the fact that, following the devastation wrought to minor lines in Oxfordshire and the South Midlands after 1963, Banbury was, overnight, somewhat oversized for its sharply reduced level of service. However, in contrast to the drastic downsizing of so many stations in the wake of the Beeching Report – a pruning which left both stations and tracks across Britain struggling to take advantage of the encouraging increase in railway traffic during the 1980s and 1990s – Banbury was perfectly able to cope with the turnaround generated by the resurgence of demand from the mid-1980s. The opportunities afforded by Banbury's architecture were evident to the station's new owners, Chiltern Railways, in 1996, if not to the British Rail of 1966: railways needed investment in future provision, and not just in that of the present.

The optimism of the Modernisation Plan also infected the new Eastern Region stations of the era – Broxbourne in Hertfordshire (Fig 7.5) and Harlow Town in Essex (Fig 7.6) – although with less spectacular results than seen at the contemporary Oxford Road. Harlow Town, built in 1960 by Paul Hamilton, John Bicknell and Ian Fraser of BR's Eastern Region (whose architectural office was then presided over by chief architect H H Powell), was horizontally conceived, whereas Oxford Road and Banbury had been vertical in their emphasis, and made much use of brick facings rather than more innovative solutions such as glazed walls or timber shells. At Harlow, the prominent concrete lift towers provided the only upward visual weight, while great use was made of light grey and blue brick clad-

Fig 7.2
Brave New City: London Midland Region's new Station at Coventry of 1962. (RO/04006/007)

Fig 7.3
W R Headley's magnificent
Manchester Oxford Road,
of 1960.
(AA97/03814)

Fig 7.4
Western Region's impressive
new Banbury Station.
This expansive, steel-and-
glass structure, opened in
1959, replaced a modest,
undersized brick building.
(RO/07285/013)

ding. However, timber and glass were far from absent: the soffit of every canopy was clad in varnished softwood boarding, while below the continuous clerestory glazing the interior walls of the concourse and booking hall were finished in pale blue glass mosaic and the concourse columns in black mosaic. In addition, as at Headley's Coventry, the station concourse was made double-height – a welcome element which provided light, space and drama (qualities which the station architects of the following decade signally failed to deliver). *The Architects' Journal* of 15 December 1960 found much to like about Harlow Town – 'The railway station is as a punctuation mark in a linear system at the point at which it meets the outside

world. Few if any modern stations convey this idea so well as Harlow Town'[3] – while the second, 1965 edition of Nikolaus Pevsner's guide to *The Buildings of England: Essex* applauded it as 'low, crisp and ungimmicky'.[4] The station was subsequently listed Grade II in 1996, English Heritage's list description opining that:

Under H H Powell, with his principal assistant Roger Walters, the Eastern Region Architect's Department was the most creative branch of British Railways, designing a number of powerful modern stations in conjunction with the Region's electrification. The new station for Harlow New Town was the flagship of this achievement. It is a building with powerful spatial qualities, of especial interest particularly for its architectural design.[5]

Fig 7.5
Broxbourne, Hertfordshire.
(DP158550)

Fig 7.6
Harlow Town of 1960.
(DP159598)

Nearby Broxbourne Station of 1959–61 – rebuilt and resited as part of the electrification of the Liverpool Street–Bishop's Stortford line, another key Modernisation Plan project – was designed in a similar vein, although here the project architect was the South African-trained

Peter Rainiers working under John Ward, who became Powell's successor as head of architecture for BR's Eastern Region. At Broxbourne the reinforced concrete frame was brutally exposed as floor and roof slabs, while the purple brick-clad lift towers rose from asymmetrically spaced island platforms to support the ample bridge. Again, a double-height booking hall was provided, and the ceilings lined in timber; this time, though, the entrance elevation was fully glazed. English Heritage's listing inspector later judged this station as ...

one of the most powerfully composed stations of the period, a development of the plan already adopted by the same Regional architects for Harlow Station using a more forceful profile and simpler contrast of masses and materials. Critically well-received at the time of completion, this is one of a very small number of post-war railway stations of clear architectural distinction.[6]

More radical than Harlow or Broxbourne was John Ward's own Barking of 1959–61 (Fig 7.7). Here, Ward designed a large, 14-bay, glazed booking hall covered with an undulating, trussed concrete roof cantilevered over the entrance as an awning. The model was clearly the recent, celebrated station of Rome Termini, completed in 1950 and designed by Eugenio Montuori and his colleagues. Even the long concourse was, as at Rome, installed transversely behind the glazed entrance (which is

Fig 7.7
Barking of 1959-61.
(RO/19122/007)

Fig 7.8
*N G T Wikeley's bright, light
and airy new station at
Chichester of 1960.*
(RO/05896/003)

now, inevitably, full of retail outlets). Barking and Rome made unlikely twins but, in Ward's hands, the new Essex station was as bold and assured as that at the Eternal City, with no trace of a cultural cringe. Pevsner, for one, was delighted: his *Essex* volume of 1965 called Barking 'unquestionably one of the best English stations of this date',[7] and it was subsequently listed.

Barking was not the only inspiring medium-sized station of the 1960s. At Chichester (Fig 7.8), of 1961, Southern Region's architect, N G T Wikeley, brought the whole entrance hall to clerestory height and gave it an entirely glazed wall in the manner of Banbury. Wikeley's

Folkestone Central of 1968 was, however, less impressive; here the heavily emphasized slab roof bore heavily down on the perfunctory entrance openings, while the feeble and cursory northern tower – so much less muscular than the vast concrete beams which supported the long, low entrance ramp approaching the main elevation from the east – looked like an undersized afterthought. Certainly Folkestone's low, dark, ground-floor concourse does not encourage exploration today. Far more assured was Wikeley's 1961 rebuilding of Hurst Green, with its simple but well-signed glazed entrance bay and low wings – both of which have now, sadly, been mangled beyond recognition.

Setting a bad example

Disappointingly, the stimulating new exemplars provided by the radical, airy modernism of Coventry and Oxford Road did not become the templates of the future. More stations seemed to follow the example set not by Banbury or Barking, but by the cynically rebuilt new termini at Euston and Birmingham New Street – abandoning any attempt at originality, animation or (God forbid) beauty in the quest for a cost-effective and low-maintenance environment. Ironically, these buildings were also, within 30 years, visibly failing both in terms of everyday use and structural integrity. The fact that they looked just like any other office block also meant that, for many would-be rail passengers, the station – and its services – vanished into its urban context.

Euston

The tragedy of the new Euston was not just that P C Hardwick's Great Hall was demolished and his father's iconic Euston Arch needlessly sacrificed, but that the station's much-vaunted replacement was so depressingly mediocre. The airiness and confidence that W R Headley and his department imparted to Coventry and other, smaller stations on the LMR network was signally lacking at Euston. Notoriously, the marble-floored concourse featured no passenger seating – a curiously over-optimistic attitude in the Age of Beeching – while the ramps down to the tracks were found to be unusable by disabled travellers. Perhaps the stultifying lack of imagination shown in the treatment of both exteriors and interiors can be at least partly blamed on the consultant architects with whom Headley and his staff were forced into partnership: Seifert and Partners, the *eminences grises* of bland commercial modernism. As if to hide their embarrassment, British Rail ensured that the lacklustre, overly horizontal block which resulted from this marriage of convenience was hidden from the main road by a trio of insipid office blocks, under which cowered a disgracefully perfunctory 'bus station', and whose bulk necessitated a forest of signage to help the weary visitor to actually identify and reach the station. The Euston Arch it definitely wasn't. And only 40 years after it was opened, the railways and the government were promoting its demolition. While the recession of 2009–11 stopped these proposals in

their tracks, the launching in 2012 of the ambitious 'HS2' scheme – designed to link London, Birmingham and the North with a dedicated high-speed line which would emanate from a rebuilt Euston – seemed to spell the end of the line for the most underwhelming terminus in London.

Birmingham New Street

LMR's replacement New Street Station at Birmingham was even worse. British planners have long dreamed of exploiting the air rights over major railway stations, in the manner that had become common in America – and which had, famously, done for one of the most impressive and successful of the world's termini, New York's Pennsylvania Station of 1905–10, and which now threatened the survival of that Beaux Arts masterpiece, the same city's legendary Grand Central Station of 1910–13. A vast tower block was ultimately built on Grand Central's north side, but the fledgling conservation movement of the 1970s prevented the rest of the station being overwhelmed by an even bigger tower. Birmingham was not so lucky: the city council used the excuse of the wartime bomb damage to the celebrated trainshed to demolish all traces of the Victorian station – along, as we have seen, with the adjacent Queen's Hotel – and to bury a new interchange of 1964–7, Penn Station-like, in Stygian gloom under a retail and residential development of breathtaking vapidity. The LMR's project leader, Kenneth Davies, had little room to manoeuvre, and thus we should perhaps not be too damning of his depressing underground bunker. Less excusable were the dismal, claustrophobic corridors of the shopping centre of 1968–70 above (latterly known as 'The Pallasades') and the adjacent, nondescript, 20-storey block built by Birmingham City Architects Department (under the ostensible lead of the corrupt Alan Maudsley), which the city dared to name Stephenson Tower in an egregious insult to the Victorian engineer.

New Street found few admirers. *Country Life*'s readers voted it the second worst eyesore in the nation in 2003, while architectural historian Andy Foster, in his 2005 Pevsner guide to the city's buildings, could find nothing to say in its defence. In 2010 work started on 'Gateway Plus', a scheme to rebuild the station with a far larger concourse – one that actually let in a modicum of natural light – which involved the demolition of Maudsley's tower and the replacement of The Pallasades by a new shopping centre, titled 'Grand Central Birmingham' in a highly inappropriate nod to New York's inspiring terminus. New Street's inadequate platforms, however, will still be largely swathed in underground gloom.

Southern discomfort

The 1970s was a grim decade for the railways in general, and for stations in particular. Lack of government investment, and lack of managerial vision, saw services and fabric contract further even than Beeching had ever envisaged. All of British Rail's new regions were to some extent to blame; none more so than Southern Region, which, as we have seen, embarked from the late 1960s onwards on a wholesale pro-

gramme of demolishing fine Victorian stations. Those Southern sites which were actually provided with replacement structures were given prefabricated, single-storey buildings of no architectural distinction whatsoever. East Grinstead of 1970–1 (Fig 7.9) was a typical example of Southern's new aesthetic. Away went the engagingly detailed, five-bay brick building of 1882 (and also all of the High Level station of 1883); in its place came an anonymous box, the principal elevation of which was devoid of all interest save for a derisory 'porch'. The wealthy town of East Grinstead became increasingly embarrassed by this mean and undersized replacement, and in 2012 it was demolished to make way for a brand new station by Howard Fairbairn (Fig 7.10). With a tripartite plan, and notable for its tall, glazed booking hall (which

Fig 7.9
East Grinstead: Southern Region's grimly functional replacement station of 1970–1.
(© East Grinstead Museum, reproduced with their kind permission)

Fig 7.10
East Grinstead: Howard Fairbairn's new station of 2012.
(© Stephen Craven)

gave a perceptible nod to Holden's Sudbury Town), East Grinstead finally got the station it deserved, and the demolition of 1970 had been avenged.

East Grinstead's fate was shared by its Sussex neighbour, Uckfield, which in 1969 suddenly found itself as the terminus of the attractive Wealden Line, as services south to Lewes were cut. A local proposal to reopen the line to Lewes, the culmination of a campaign begun in 1986, was turned down in 2008 by the Department of Transport. Currently only the privately owned Lavender Line, running north from Isfield, occupies part of the closed route. The closure also meant that the fine, twin-gabled station at Uckfield of 1868 was now stranded on the wrong side of a level-crossing, making train operation in and out unnecessarily complicated. In 1991, therefore, the station was relocated to the north of the road, and temporarily housed in a Portakabin. The latter was replaced in 2010 by a simple, neat box, designed again by Howard Fairbairn (who had also been commissioned by Southern to build the new station at Hastings: see Fig 8.10), as part of Network Rail's National Station Improvement Scheme (NSIP). Not only did the station's resiting appear to be the death knell for the campaign to reopen the Wealden Line; the fine, original Victorian building was itself unnecessarily demolished in December 2000.

East Grinstead's new station of 1971 had been built according to the CLASP (Consortium of Local Authorities Special Programme) prefabricated system. CLASP had been devised in 1957 to provide school buildings rapidly and cheaply. It was subsequently extended to replacement railway stations, such as at Ditton and the larger St Helens Shaw Street (Fig 7.11), later St Helens Central, of 1961. However, the resulting modular stations were not only relentlessly horizontal and uninspiringly anonymous; they were also generally too small for existing traffic, let alone able to cope with any future increases in custom. Ditton assured its footnote in the annals of railway history by becoming the first station to be closed by the newly privatised British Railways (then known as Railtrack) in 1994. At St Helens, the basic CLASP structure had been improved by being topped by a tall, glazed clerestory with a dihedral roof – a feature befitting the home town of Pilkington's Glass, which was soon advertising itself on the clerestory's front elevation. However, even this attribute did not save the building. Demolished

in 2005, it was replaced on an adjacent site by an impressive new station by SBS Architects of Manchester, comprising a curved, glazed concourse dominated by a soaring, twin-finned, copper-clad entrance.

Southern Region enthusiastically seized the opportunities offed by the CLASP system, and initiated a wholesale programme of replacing good Victorian stations, with many decades if not centuries of life left in them, with CLASP boxes. In use, however, the new structures proved both fragile as well as undersized, and few still stand today. At Crayford in Kent in 1968, the handsome, weatherboarded Victorian station was replaced with a CLASP shed, which in turn gave way to a nondescript, pedimented brick structure when the CLASP block rapidly burned to the ground in 2000. The Victorian stations at Fleet in Hampshire, Aylesham in Kent, and Belmont, Ashtead and Berrylands in Surrey – to name but five – were all replaced by CLASP units in 1968–9. At Charlton, in south-east London, the dismal CLASP block of 1968 (Fig 7.12) was at least augmented by the provision of dihedral, cantilevered concrete platform canopies.

Hampton Wick's fine brick building of 1863 (Fig 7.13), with its prominent arched windows, also succumbed to Southern's campaign of thoughtless destruction; yet its replacement CLASP station was itself eventually supplanted by a classically inspired, glazed box-temple at the turn of the century. Poole's miserable CLASP buildings did not even last 20 years before they were substituted by a more imaginative if still rather temporary-looking structure, whose concrete roof comprised an engaging sweep of vast, linked segmental arches. In 2004 this station, too, was nominated for replacement, though at the time of writing none of the ambitious schemes intended to create a new transport hub for Poole have won the requisite funding.

As the 1970s progressed, new stations became increasingly brutalist, and the light, airy glazed forms of 1960 were replaced by heavy structures with emphatic slab roofs. Thus, while the Southern Region's Maze Hill of 1972 (Fig 7.14) was a pleasingly proportioned glazed box (whose adaptation for modern technology has now resulted in the filling-in of the second tier of glazing), the large, blank glazed structure built at the resited Bedford Station (Figs 7.15 and 7.16) six years later was a characterless design which could have served

Fig 7.11
St Helens Shaw Street.
(Taken from David A
Ingham collection, original
photographer unknown)

Fig 7.12
Charlton: the appalling
station entrance of 1968.
(© Stephen Craven)

as easily for a corporate headquarters as for a railway station. At Stevenage of 1973 – where the station was moved a mile to the north to serve the New Town – four brick lift towers gave prominence and weight to what was otherwise another nondescript, horizontal building. LMR's Birmingham International of 1976, however, resorted to the horizontalised slab roof – a feature which has dated the building very quickly. The same architectural office did better at the large new station at Milton Keynes of 1982 (Fig 7.17): here, the tall, glazed concourse did at least try to mimic the aspirational height of Headley's Coventry up the line. But Milton Keynes's entrance remained anonymous and apologetic, and the ambience of the building is

one of a shopping centre rather than a station. Far worse was the new Gloucester Station of 1977, which replaced the functions of both the Great Western Railway's (GWR) old Gloucester Central and the Midland Railway's Gloucester Eastgate, with no attempt to evoke a railway aesthetic. Its lumpen block, built alongside the second-longest platform in Britain, was indistinguishable from any other dismal corporate structure. Its lack of imagination and ambition appeared to mirror the new railway reality of Gloucester's location: once an important railway junction, the city was now marooned to the west of the Birmingham–Bristol main line.

The 1970s and 1980s represented the nadir of Britain's railway culture, both in terms of

Fig 7.13
Hampton Wick: senselessly
demolished.
(RO/22235/001)

Fig. 7.14
Maze Hill, of 1972.
(BB99/09371)

Fig 7.15
Bedford: the demolished
Gothic station.
(OP01408)

Fig 7.16
Bedford's characterless new
station.
(Taken from
http://commons.wikimedia.
org/wiki/)

the lack of investment in the railways and in the dismissive attitude to the network's architectural assets. Few new stations were built, and those that were constructed were not just of a depressingly uninspired standard but were irrationally downsized. Oxford (which admittedly had never boasted a GWR station of any architectural merit) was, in 1971–4, provided with a mean, low main building and robbed of its third main-line platform – a senseless loss which British Rail's Western Region was soon to regret, as Oxford became a notorious bottleneck. The new station at Peterborough, of 1983, and Telford Central (Fig 7.18), of 1986, were both too small to handle any growth in custom, and also featured 1970s-style slab roofs which epitomised commercial modernism at its most lowering and lifeless. Peterborough additionally boasted tall brick lift towers in the vein of Stevenage – albeit 10 years had passed since the latter was opened. It was no surprise that the parsimonious booking hall area at Peterborough quickly found itself drastically undersized for main-line operation in a rapidly expanding city. In 2012 the booking hall and concourse area was accordingly rebuilt by London archi-

tects ColladoCollins on far more spacious and audacious lines, with passengers now entering an oval concourse under a large 'flying canopy' and through a rectangular, purple gateway (Fig 7.19). It may not be the Euston Arch, but the dramatic new entrance to Peterborough does show that railway station architecture is back on track.

The few major station projects which were pursued in the 1970s and 1980s largely involved the exploitation of the air rights of existing sites, in the manner of Birmingham New Street. During the 1980s, Hawkshaw's trainshed at Charing Cross was covered by an immense retail and office development, designed in a bold postmodern idiom by Terry Farrell and Partners; Cannon Street was buried beneath a vast office complex and sports centre, by BDP – a scheme which at least saw the removal of John Poulson's lifeless block of 20 years earlier; and, most scandalously, Sir George Berkeley's Fenchurch Street was demolished behind its main façade to make way for an office development by Fitzroy Robinson. The only air-rights scheme which displayed any imagination or sympathy for the historic

Fig 7.18
The dismally uninspired
station at Telford Central
of 1986.
(© John Horton)

stations was Liverpool Street, remodelled after 1985 to make way for Rosehaugh Stanhope's gigantic, American-styled Broadgate complex at the eastern edge of the City of London. Here, at least, the new development was consigned to the rear of the concourse, which was allowed to admit an encouraging amount of natural light and to celebrate Edward Wilson's fine brickwork and ironwork. Indeed, the new scheme finally made sense of what had always – as we have already seen – been a notoriously difficult station to navigate, even if much of the Victorian ambience of Wilson's muddled building was inevitably lost, banished by the gleaming white surfaces of the many new retail units (Fig 7.20).

Today, reassuringly, the air-rights lobby is far weaker than it was in the dark days of the 1960s, 1970s and 1980s. A revealing litmus test of this welcome transition came in the early years of the 21st century, when Network Rail – successor from 2002 to Railtrack, which had

Fig 7.19
Peterborough: the new
entrance.
(© Network Rail)

taken over the rump of British Rail's network responsibilities – proposed crushing the fourth, northernmost span of the trainshed at Paddington beneath an oversized, Brobdignagian office development by Nicholas Grimshaw & Partners. Span 4, as it was known, had been sensitively built between 1908 and 1914 by the GWR to match Brunel's original, tripartite trainshed; the company's chief engineer, one W Armstrong, even reproduced the star-shaped perforations on Brunel's iron beams. However, while this structure might well have

disappeared in the 1960s or 1970s, an energetic campaign led by the Victorian Society and SAVE Britain's Heritage ensured its survival. In the event it was not demolished but conserved, between 2009 and 2011. Revealingly, when in 2005 Network Rail announced it intended to provide modern concourse facilities at King's Cross, a lucrative air-rights development over the venerable trainshed was never contemplated; instead, John McAslan designed a soaring new concourse to the west of the Victorian station.

8

A new railway age

After decades of underinvestment and diminishing expectations, the 1990s saw a dramatic turnaround in the fortunes of Britain's railways. A crucial element of this revival derived from the railway companies' belated realisation that inspiring new stations, rather than minimalist, functional boxes, would attract new and repeat custom, and would help to restore the railway station to its rightful place as a social focus for the community, a reassuring meeting place for visitors, and a glamorous catalyst for urban regeneration.

The age of the train

The standard bearer for the new era in station design in Britain was the large extension added by Nicholas Grimshaw and Partners, between 1989 and 1993, to London's giant Waterloo terminus (Fig 8.1). In the context of the capital's other principal termini – stations such as Paddington, King's Cross and St Pancras – Waterloo was architecturally undistinguished. Indeed, as noted above, the government have so far refused to list the building. Originally constructed in 1848, Waterloo was rebuilt by the London and South Western Railway (LSWR) between 1901 and 1922 in a scheme which saw the removal of the famous Necropolis Station, explicitly designed to serve the vast cemetery at Brookwood in Surrey, together with the adjacent brothel, and the addition of J R Scott's splendid Victory Arch. Now Grimshaw added to the north a banana-shaped extension, Waterloo International, to house the continental Eurostar services which linked London with Paris and Brussels from 1994. Grimshaw's stand-alone, 400m (1312ft) trainshed was, like the site itself, dramatically curved, with its glass roof supported by blue-painted, bowstring-shaped steel trusses. Structural glass played a key role, with vast sheets extending down to track level and glass fins being employed as

beams. On arrival in 1994 international passengers were greeted by the engaging sight of Jean-Luc Vilmouth's ceiling fish sculptures gently undulating in the breezes. Sadly, these amusing adornments were soon removed and, after Eurostar's services had been moved into the revamped St Pancras in 2007, Grimshaw's

Fig 8.1
London Waterloo:
Grimshaw's Eurostar
terminus.
(BB93/26573)

fine building was mothballed. South West Trains occasionally made use of the southernmost platform (Platform 20) but, inexplicably, no use was made of the rest of the international platforms – whose spacious basement departure concourse appeared an obvious candidate for conversion to retail use. In 2012 it was proposed that the international terminus serve as the London destination of all the country's (now shamefully few) sleeper trains; but at the time of writing little has been done to further this concept.

While St Pancras had been ostensibly saved by its Grade I listing in 1967, the station's future was, until the late 1990s, still disturbingly uncertain. In 1978 British Rail lobbied to have Scott's fine booking hall replaced by a modern travel centre, and was only prevented from doing so by a public enquiry – which prompted *Private Eye*'s notorious fake press advertisement, purportedly putting the case for the wrecking of 'this horrible, tatty old Victorian pile' on behalf of British Rail (whose slogan was altered to: 'Only to be used in an emergency').[1] In 1980, a disgruntled British Rail pulled its own staff out of the decaying building in an act of petty spite; eight years later the last office worker left the building. By the early 1990s the empty hotel was in a poor condition. Safeguarding works by Margaret Davies of 1993–5 at least ensured the roof was made watertight,

and also revealed once more some of the stunning, original decoration of the Grand Staircase as well as tantalising glimpses behind the grey paint surfaces of the earlier schemes for the public spaces and hotel rooms. In 1998 the station's new owners, London and Continental Railways (L&C), named RHWL as architects for the conversion of the hotel and offices to a 'hotel with loft apartments'. Although L&C collapsed two weeks after this announcement, the government swiftly conjured a new consortium – 50 per cent owned by SNCF and SNCB, the French and Belgian national railway operators – to ensure the completion of both the St Pancras development, and the creation of the nation's first high-speed railway line ('HS1') to link the station with the Channel Tunnel.

The reborn St Pancras of 2007 (Fig 8.2) was a marvellous achievement, one which showed how powerful great railway stations could be as agents of urban renewal as well as advertisements for the glamour of railway travel. Barlow and Ordish's soaring iron roof, painted sky blue (and now extending northwards in a disarmingly functional idiom), now presided over the comings and goings of Eurostar trains to France and Belgium as well as the more prosaic services to the Midlands. Adjacent to the Eurostar platforms, the developers optimistically installed the longest champagne bar in the world (they clearly did not intend the trainshed

Fig 8.2
St Pancras: the trainshed reborn. Martin Jennings's inspired statue of Sir John Betjeman looks on.
(DP095751)

to become a haunt of trainspotters); this in turn was soon complemented by Martin Jennings's evocative sculpture of Sir John Betjeman, whose Victorian Society had done so much to save this important building from disfigurement and demolition. The former Booking Hall – almost destroyed in 1978 – was sympathetically converted into an upmarket bar, while the Midland Grand next door arose anew as a luxurious hotel and ultra-premium apartments. Below, in the space between Barlow and Ordish's enormous tie-concourse and the actual ground floor, where Burton beer barrels once rested after their traumatic journey from the Midlands, now shoppers and office workers circulated around retail units and restaurants, while Eurostar passengers checked into their (surprisingly undersized and ill-equipped) departure area. The inadequacy of the departure lounge aside, the only really jarring note at the new St Pancras was the installation at the south end of the trainshed of a giant sculpture, *The Meeting Place* by Paul Day, whose scale and composition made such a grating contrast with both Barlow and Ordish's shed and with Jennings's sensitively modelled evocation of Betjeman.

As the 20th century neared the buffers, other large English stations also began to prosper once more. Whilst sited only a mile to the west of St Pancras, Marylebone could boast none of the architectural opulence or inspiring scale of Scott, Barlow and Ordish's Gothic extravaganza. However, the success of Network SouthEast in the 1990s – in 1993 Marylebone services reached the West Midlands for the first time since 1967 – and the ability of Chiltern Railways to capitalise on this excellent start after 1996, provided the impetus for the remodelling of what, in the 1970s and 1980s, had been a dark, depressing suburban terminus – one which British Rail had, between 1983 to 1984, proposed for closure. By Peter Parker's plan of 1983, Marylebone was to have been converted into a coach station at the end of a 'high-speed bus way'. Closure notices were even posted at Marylebone in 1984. Today, Marylebone's bustle and colour testifies to the revitalisation of the railways, and consequently of the destinations they serve, in the 21st century.

St Pancras and Marylebone were not the only great stations to profit from the belated acknowledgement of the architectural and social significance of the railway station. At Paddington, 'The Lawn' (the area between

Fig 8.3
King's Cross: McAslan's breathtaking new concourse.
(DP149034)

the main concourse and the hotel entrance) was rebuilt and extended between 2005 and 2006, whilst Network Rail's plan to demolish the shed's fourth span was, as we have seen, successfully opposed. At King's Cross, the disfiguring front apron of 1972, which had long obscured Cubitt's powerful brick arches, was finally removed in 2012, and new services inserted in a new Western Concourse – a magnificent structure by John McAslan & Partners covered with a fabulous, lacework iron roof (Fig 8.3). This superb new concourse, which won a slew of awards between 2012 and 2013, was soon complemented by a splendid pub carved out of the former royal mail depot at the new concourse's north end.

Beyond the capital

Outside London, the pace of inventive and occasionally visionary development – architecture very much in the spirit of the railway architects of the Victorian age – also steamed ahead in the new century. Peterborough, as we have seen, was provided with a more heroic entrance. In 2002 the former Midland railway station at Sheffield was rebuilt, and in 2009 opened what swiftly became a multi-award-winning pub in the former First Class Lounge of 1904 on Platform 1. Manchester Piccadilly was remodelled between 1997 and 2007, gaining a new glazed entrance, while in 2013, as we have seen, work began on a £44 million scheme to restore and extend its long-neglected cousin at Victoria. The belated opening of Britain's first high-speed railway provided the impetus not only for the construction of a new station at Ashford in Kent of 1994–5, but also its imaginative rebuilding in 2009 by Frankham (Fig 8.4). The old station was finally swept away in 1999, but in truth all but two platform awnings of 1908 had already disappeared in the ruth-

less reconstruction which had been executed to coincide with the Kent electrification scheme of 1962. At Leeds, the trainshed and concourse were rebuilt on a grander and more imaginative scale in 2002 by Mackellar Architecture, while in 2011 the city council unveiled a £14 million development which would create a dramatic new southern entrance for the station. And, as already noted, between 2012 and 2013 the mean-spirited 1960s station at Wakefield Westgate was demolished and rebuilt a few yards further north. The new station, designed by CJCT Architects of Leeds working with master-planners the Buckingham Group, was far more capacious than its miserly predecessor (Fig 8.5). Instead of blank brick or white-tiled walls, the passenger was now greeted by an undulating glass curtain wall fronting a large, partially grassed open space.

Westgate's transformation focused attention on the city's other principal station. Wakefield Kirkgate was originally built in 1840 by Francis Thompson for the Manchester and Leeds Railway (which was subsumed into the Lancashire and Yorkshire in 1847), but was rebuilt in 1854

Fig 8.4
Ashford International: the interior of 2009.
(JPL01/10/61726
© English Heritage.
John Laing Collection)

Fig 8.5
*The new Wakefield
Westgate.
(© East Coast)*

– possibly with the architectural advice of G T Andrews, even though Andrews had largely withdrawn from the architectural profession following the disgrace of his patron, George Hudson, after 1849. The handsome, classical, stone-built principal (northern) elevation of 1854 was dominated by a tall, pedimented clock tower, which was linked to three-bay pavilions by single-storey wings. In 1972, however, the deteriorating station was partly demolished: the principal casualty was the fine iron trainshed, with the remaining historic fabric being pared back so that all the service pipes and wires could now be seen. An insensitive modern canopy was later squeezed onto the northern platform.

Kirkgate's future remained uncertain even after it was listed in 1979 (Figs 8.6, 8.7 and 8.8). Its booking hall facilities were removed, most of its surrounding signage was taken down, and a new housing estate built immediately in front of its entrance. What remained of the original structure on the southernmost platform was crudely converted into a subway entrance, with oversized windows. In January 2008 the former goods warehouse was demolished to make way for a depot and, later that year, the external station wall collapsed, destroying a parked car. By 2009 the station had become notorious as a hub for criminal activity of all kinds, and following his visit there in July of that year was branded by the then Transport Minister, Lord Adonis, as 'the worst "medium-large" station in Britain'.[2] By 2012, even the pub opposite the station entrance was derelict, and buses no longer bothered to stop there. In 2012, however, Wakefield Council finally unveiled a comprehensive development scheme which would restore the station's fabric and introduce a café, offices, meeting rooms and shops. Kirkgate was now to be made the hub of an ambitious scheme to regenerate the whole area – to which the city hoped to lure thousands of visitors following the high-profile opening of the Hepworth Gallery, located just across the river from Kirkgate Station, in 2011.

Fig 8.6
Wakefield Kirkgate today.
(© Network Rail)

Fig 8.7 (below)
Wakefield Kirkgate: in its
heyday.
(RO/06609/002)

Fig 8.8 (bottom)
Wakefield Kirkgate: at its
nadir c 1990.
(© Network Rail)

Improvements continue apace at other major stations across England. At Liverpool Lime Street, between 2007 and 2009, the dismal office block which obscured the station's main elevation was demolished and a new public plaza constructed to provide an excellent view of both the superb trainshed of 1867–74 and the southern façade of Waterhouse's Great North Western Hotel, now part of Liverpool John Moores University. From 2012, Reading Station was completely rebuilt by Grimshaw (as Nick Grimshaw's practice was now known), with six new platforms, a spectacular new overbridge and a new, glazed entrance (Fig 8.9), but retaining the original, brick Grade II-listed station by Michael Lane of 1865–7. In 2013, speculative work even began on an as-yet unfunded project to enlarge and redevelop the perennially overcrowded and under-equipped station at Oxford, a notorious operational bottleneck made far worse by the unnecessary excising of the western platform as a result of Western Region's mean-minded 'modernisation' of 1971.

Regeneration and preservation

Entirely new stations also began to appear after the millennium, designed with an imagination and ambition not seen since on Britain's railways since the 1930s. SBS Manchester's

Fig 8.9
Grimshaw's new Reading
Station.
(© Network Rail)

St Helens Central Station in Lancashire (formerly St Helens and, after 1949, St Helens Shaw Street) of 2005 and Howard Fairbairn's Hastings in East Sussex of 2004 (Fig 8.10) – the latter characterised by Fairbairn's trademark lofty glazed box and emphasised cornice, which in this case doubled as a second porch – showed how towns could use a high-profile new station as the focus for regeneration. It was not Fairbairn's fault that the Hastings scheme involved, as part of the Hopkins masterplan, the demolition of Hastings's excellent Southern Region station of 1931 – built under James Robb Scott's aegis but possibly, as we have seen, at least partly designed by the modernist pioneer E Maxwell Fry (who left the Southern for private practice in 1930). That such a fine building should be lost as recently as 2004, whatever the fine qualities of its replacement, remains a disgrace.

Fig 8.10
Hastings Station, of 2004.
Sadly, the town had already
demolished its fine interwar
station.
(Taken from
http://en.wikipedia.org/
*wiki/Hastings_railway_*
station)

Whilst exhilarating new stations are rising across the country, and plans mature to reopen destinations marooned by Beeching's over-drastic pruning of the 1960s, many fine old stations also survive in private hands – not just as homes or as hotel accommodation, but in heritage railway use. The handsome Gothic station at Minehead in Somerset of 1874, denuded of railway services in 1971, was reopened only five years later as the terminus and headquarters of the West Somerset Railway. The well-proportioned building at Horsted Keynes of 1883, with its tile-hung, jettied stationmaster's house and half-timbered porch, is now, fittingly, the headquarters of the hugely successful Bluebell Railway (Fig 8.11). The

Fig 8.11
The Bluebell Railway's
Horsted Keynes station
today.
(Photograph provided by
horstedkeynes.com)

Fig 8.12
Loughborough Central
today, restored to its 1950s
appearance by the Great
Central Railway.
(© Alan Kitching)

London, Brighton and South Coast Railway's (LBSCR) Lewes line was short-sightedly closed beyond East Grinstead in 1958; but the first, privately run Bluebell Railway trains were running from Horsted Keynes even before the Beeching Report went to press. The Lavender Line now operates from the doubled-gabled brick station at Isfield, East Sussex, of 1858, while the twin-gabled station at Alresford, Hampshire, of 1865 is the terminus of the Mid-Hants Railway's Watercress Line. The splendid Tudor station at Dereham, with its grid windows and four-centred arches, was closed in 1969 and later gutted in a fire; following excellent restoration, however, it was reopened in 2005 as one of the jewels of the privately run Mid-Norfolk Railway. The large island station at Loughborough Central of 1899 now houses the headquarters of the Great Central Railway (GCR), and has been splendidly and atmospherically reinterpreted in its 1950s guise (Fig 8.12). The small GCR station down the line at Quorn has, in contrast, been restored as it was in the 1940s, complete with a wonderfully evocative NAAFI canteen under the road bridge. In Somerset, the handsome stone building at Midsomer Norton of 1874 (Figs 8.13 and 8.14) (latterly renamed Midsomer Norton South), which was immortalised in Flanders and Swann's musical

lamentation 'The Slow Train' two years before it was closed in 1966, today hosts the burgeoning Somerset and Dorset Railway Heritage Trust. Further north, G T Andrews's stations at Pickering and Grosmont of 1847 similarly prosper as the principal stations on the North York Moors Railway (NYMR). Pickering's splendid overall roof, needlessly demolished in the 1960s, was recreated by the largely volunteer-run NYMR

Fig 8.13 (above)
Midsomer Norton South
c 1900.
(RO/07126/001)

Fig 8.14 (below)
Midsomer Norton South
today.
(© Mike Smith)

Fig 8.15
Pickering Station today.
(© Nick Fletcher)

Fig 8.16
Swanage in its last days as a
British Rail terminus.
(Taken from David A
Ingham collection, original
photographer unknown)

50 years later, and justly earned a National Railway Heritage Award in 2012 (Fig 8.15). In Dorset, the Purbeck stone façades of Swanage Station, of 1885, also play host to a thriving heritage operation: the Swanage Railway which, after both line and station were closed by BR in 1972, began reconstructing the branch's line and infrastructure. Swanage Station's 1938 platform canopy is now restored (Fig 8.16), and in March 2013 the main-line link to the eccentric Tudorbethan station of 1886 at Wareham was resurrected, enabling passage of the first Bournemouth to Swanage passenger train since 1972.

The Swanage branch is by no means the only Beeching casualty to have been revived in recent years. Between 1993 and 1998 East Midlands Trains reopened the stations on the so-called 'Robin Hood Line', restoring services to the substantial towns of Worksop – and its fine, listed Jacobean station by the MSLR's J Drabble of 1850 (Fig 8.17) – and Mansfield, which still retains its listed classical station of 1875, although one whole side together with its fine overall roof have gone. Mansfield had been plagued with the dubious distinction of being the largest town in Britain with no railway service whatsoever after the Beeching cuts, having lost both its Midland and Great Central stations in the 1960s. It is the former Midland station which survives; like most of its Great Central/ London and North Eastern Railway (LNER)

cousins, Mansfield Central – an admittedly severe, four-storey design of that austere year, 1917 – was swiftly closed, being demolished in 1972. The importance of listing was demonstrated by the fact that the reopened Robin Hood Line was able to press its protected station buildings back into everyday railway use after a gap of 30 years.

Much of the renewed interest in and reinvigoration of England's railway stations over the last 30 years would not have been possible without the support and activities of the National Railway Heritage Trust (NRHT), created in 1985 and today funded by both Network Rail and the Highways Agency. Thanks to the NRHT, the number of railway buildings and structures listed in 1985 in England, Scotland and Wales increased from 681 in 1985 to roughly 1,650 in 2013. The Trust has also acted as a watchdog for proposed alterations to existing stations, commenting on significant cases to English Heritage and local planning departments, and has additionally sought to identify new uses and owners for redundant historic station buildings. Equally significantly, the NRHT has grant-aided worthy station conservation or refurbishment projects; since 1985, the Trust has awarded over 1,300 grants, worth £41 million, to projects across the UK.

In order to recognise the best of these schemes, we now have the welcome conduit of the National Railway Heritage Awards.

Fig 8.17
Worksop, of 1850,
photographed a century
later.
(RO/21957/001)

Modestly launched in 1979, with the aim of 'encouraging and rewarding best practice in the restoration and continued upkeep of our rich heritage of railway and tramway buildings and structures',[3] its accolades are now much sought-after by developers as well as conservationists, and are widely publicised in the national media. In 2013 the award winners ranged from McAslan's inspiring new concourse at King's Cross to the restored urban interchange at Crystal Palace, rejuvenated as a terminus for the London Overground, and the impressive heritage railway stations of the GCR's Loughborough Central and the NYMR's Pickering.

As a result of the sterling work of the NRHT, of the national amenity societies, of Britain's new railway companies, and of the countless volunteers who plan and operate the nation's burgeoning heritage railways, the future for England's stations is incomparably rosier than it was 50 years ago, during the network nadir of the 1960s (Fig 8.18). Richard Beeching and Ernest Marples – along with most of the much-abused rail passengers of the 1960s and 1970s – would be astonished at the sea change in services and stations. The railway network is busier now than at any time since the 1920s. The number of railway services – one of the most sustainable forms of transport available in these ecologically aware times – is rising. Governments have been persuaded to invest in the railways, rather than to divert badly needed funding to the roads. And more disused lines and abandoned stations are being brought back into service every year.

The key part that railways, and railway stations, can play in contemporary society is now freely acknowledged not just by railway companies and their passengers but also, implicitly, in the vast increase in the number of railway buildings which now enjoy statutory protection. This security – which is, admittedly, often only as strong as the local authority's will to enforce it – has, as noted above, enabled many fine historic stations to experience a well-deserved new lease of life. All over the country, derelict station sites are being resuscitated not merely to function as a much-needed public transport resource but also to serve as the focus for community life and for urban, or indeed rural, renewal. The railway station has now become a symbol of both the past *and* the future.

Fig 8.18
Petworth Station: rebuilt in 1892, closed in 1955, and now serving as a bed-and-breakfast hotel.
(Photograph provided by The Old Railway Station www.old-station.co.uk)

GLOSSARY

acroteria: ornaments (single: *acroterion*) projecting from the apex or corners of a pediment or entablature, usually in the form of a 'palmette' leaf.

architrave: the architectural frame of a door or window or, in classical architecture, the lowest element of the entablature, derived from a lintel.

attic: the topmost part of a classical façade, situated above the cornice.

Beaux Arts: a heavy, academic, Roman-influenced neoclassical style of architecture, made popular in the USA at the end of the 19th century.

bracket: an architectural support, usually decorated (if made of wood or plaster) or pierced (if of metal).

clerestory: an upper level of a building which is pierced by many windows to let in light.

colonnade: a long row of columns.

concourse: a covered circulation space, usually placed (in a railway station) in front of or above the platforms.

curtilage: the immediate area around a building.

dado: the lower part of a wall, between the dado (or chair) rail and the skirting board, corresponding to the plinth of a column.

dihedral roof: a roof created from more than two planes or ridges.

Doric: the most severe of the original three Greek orders of architecture, with square capitals and columns without bases.

Dutch gable: a gable with hips and undulating curves, sometimes terminating in a pediment.

entablature: the superstructure resting on columns or pilasters in classical architecture, comprising the architrave, frieze and (at the top) the cornice.

faience: tin-glazed earthenware. Faience tiles were often used on station walls in the nineteenth century.

finial: decorative element marking the termination of a roof, spire, dome or other architectural element.

GRP: glass-reinforced plastic.

halt: small, unstaffed station with few or no buildings.

hammerbeam: a large, exposed, horizontally projecting beam, much used in large roofs in England from *c* 1300.

head-building: building at the front of larger railway termini, comprising the booking and railway offices.

in antis: columns in a wall opening, supporting the fabric above.

Ionic: the second of the three Greek orders, characterised by curled volutes, resembling rams' horns, in the capital.

Jacobean: from, or reviving, the architecture of the period of King James I (1602–25).

mansard roof: a four-sided roof whose upper slopes are more steeply pitched than the lower planes.

moderne: a style of architecture which evolved in the 1930s, combining art deco forms with elements of Continental Modernism.

Palladian: classical architecture, popular in Britian from *c* 1715, built according to a system of proportionality popularised by the Italian architect Andrea Palladio (1508–80).

pargeting: decorative plasterwork on the exterior of a building.

pediment: triangular or curved ('segmental') gable above the entablature.

pilaster: flattened column which serves no structural purpose.

porte cochère: a porch big enough for a horse and carriage to stop under.

portico: a classical porch supported by columns and often topped by a pediment.

quoin: emphasised block at the corner of a wall.

spandrel: the space between an arch and its architectural frame.

tetrastyle: a row of four columns, usually in a portico.

trainshed: an overall station roof, generally found on larger stations and invariably made of iron and glass.

truss: a combination of straight or curved wooden or iron members which, in railway architecture, supports a wide span.

valance: decorative vertical border to wooden or iron platform canopies.

NOTES

Chapter 1

1 Quoted in Scott, J 1913 *Railway Romance and Other Essays.* Edinburgh: Ballantyne, 71
2 Quoted in Parissien 1997, 7–8
3 Biddle 1973, 13
4 Meeks 1956, 35
5 Colvin 2006, 374
6 Richards and Mackenzie 1986, 19
7 Barman 1950, 16
8 Freeman 1999, 16
9 Quoted in Parissien 1997, 9
10 Quoted in Parissien 1997, 31

Chapter 2

1 Colvin 2006, 459
2 Quoted in Parissien 1997, 77–8
3 Ellaway 1994, 6
4 Brindle 2004, 40
5 Brindle 2004, 33
6 Barman 1950, 32
7 Barman 1950, 34
8 Barman 1950, 33
9 Meeks 1956, 85
10 Whishaw 1842, 368, 375
11 Meeks 1956, 45

Chapter 3

1 Richards and Mackenzie 1986, 6
2 Barman 1950, 26
3 Thomas 2011, 58
4 Thomas 2011, 43
5 Thomas 2011, 60
6 Biddle 1973, 40
7 Biddle 1973, 44

Chapter 4

1 Colvin 2006, 890
2 Quoted in Brooks, A and Pevsner, N 2007 *The Buildings of England: Worcestershire.* New Haven and London: Yale University Press, 462

3 'London, Chatham and Dover Railway', *The Building News* **10** 27. 9 January 1863
4 Biddle 1973, 151
5 Fry, M 1975 *Autobiographical Sketches*. London: Elek, 143 and passim; *see also* 'Fry, (Edwin) Maxwell' in Powers, A 2004 *The New Dictionary of National Biography.* Oxford: Oxford University Press
6 Pevsner, N 1952 *The Buildings of England: Middlesex.* Harmondsworth: Penguin, 140

Chapter 5

1 Farrell's heavy-handed intervention followed a pattern established in the mid-1980s, when George Berkeley's Fenchurch Street of 1854, built for the London, Tilbury and Southend Railway behind a splendid Italian palace front, surmounted by a huge, segmental brick arch, was façaded by Fitzroy Robinson and Arups between 1983 and 1987.
2 Biddle 1973, 121
3 Bradley 2007, 9–10
4 Bradley 2007, 76
5 Parissien 1997, 41
6 Bradley 2007, 77
7 Meeks 1956, 85
8 Biddle 1973, 127
9 Betjeman and Gay 1972, 114
10 Betjeman and Gay 1972, 30
11 Biddle 1973, 138

Chapter 6

1 Stamp himself, however, failed to survive the war: he was killed by a direct hit on the air-raid shelter in his Bromley garden in April 1941
2 Parissien 1997, 81–3
3 The others were Edward Heath, Prime Minister after 1970, and Charles Hill
4 For song lyrics *see* Richards and MacKenzie 1986, preface
5 Richards and MacKenzie 1986, 7
6 Parissien 1997, 63

7 Biddle 1973, 125
8 Foster, A 2005 *The Buildings of England: Birmingham.* New Haven and London: Yale University Press, 110

Chapter 7

1 Richards and MacKenzie 1986, 6
2 Pevsner, N 1977 *The Buildings of England: Hertfordshire,* 2 edn. Harmondsworth: Penguin, 272
3 *The Architects' Journal*, 15 December 1960, 869
4 Pevsner N 1965 *The Buildings of England: Essex*, 2 edn. Harmondsworth: Penguin, 231
5 *See* The National Heritage List for England at www.english-heritage.org.uk (accessed 26 August 2014)
6 *See* The National Heritage List for England at www.english-heritage.org.uk (accessed 26 August 2014)
7 Pevsner N 1965 *The Buildings of England: Essex*, 2 edn. Harmondsworth: Penguin, 70

Chapter 8

1 *Private Eye*, 4 August 1978
2 'Lord Adonis criticises Network Rail in letter about state of Wakefield Kirkgate'. *Wakefield Express*. Johnston Press Digital Publishing. 30 July 2009
3 Taken from the National Railway Heritage Awards website, *see* http://nrha.org.uk/ (accessed 26 August 2014)

FURTHER READING

Antell, R 1984 *Southern Country Stations: 1 – London & South Western Railway.* Hersham: Ian Allan

Barman, C 1950 *An Introduction to Railway Architecture.* London: Art & Technics

Betjeman, J and Gay, J 1972 *London's Historic Railway Stations.* London: John Murray

Biddle, G 1973 *Victorian Stations.* Newton Abbot: David & Charles

Biddle, G 1986 *Great Railway Stations of Britain.* Newton Abbot: David & Charles

Biddle, G 2003 *Britain's Historic Railway Buildings.* Oxford: Oxford University Press

Biddle, G and Nock, O S 1983 *The Railway Heritage of Britain.* London: Michael Joseph

Biddle, G and Simmons, J 1997 *The Oxford Companion to British Railway History.* Oxford: Oxford University Press

Biddle, G and Spence, J 1977 *The British Railway Station.* Newton Abbot: David & Charles

Binding, J 2001 *Brunel's Bristol Temple Meads.* Hersham: Oxford Publishing

Binney, M 1995 *Architecture of Rail.* London: Academy Editions

Binney, M and Pearce, D 1979 *Railway Architecture.* London: Bloomsbury Books

Bowers, M 1975 *Railway Styles in Building.* New Malden: Almark

Bradley, S 2007 *St Pancras Station.* London: Profile

Brindle, S 2004 *Paddington Station.* Swindon: English Heritage

Brindle, S 2013 *Paddington Station,* 2 edn. Swindon: English Heritage

Brindle, S and Cruikshank, D 2006 *Brunel: The Man Who Built the World.* Quezon City, AZ: Phoenix Publishing

Buck, G A 1992 *A Pictorial Survey of Railway Stations.* Oxford: OPC

Butt, R V J 1995 *The Directory of Railway Stations.* Sparkfold: Patrick Stephens

Clough, D N 2013 *Dr Beeching's Remedy.* Hersham: Ian Allan

Colvin, H 2006 *A Biographical Dictionary of British Architects,* 4 edn. New Haven and London: Yale University Press

Ellaway, K J 1994 *The Great British Railway Station – Euston.* Oldham: Irwell Press

Faith, N 1990 *The World the Railways Made.* London: The Bodley Head

Foster, R D 1990 *Birmingham New Street.* Didcot: Wild Swan Publications

Freeman, M 1999 *Railways and the Victorian Imagination.* New Haven and London: Yale University Press

Hendry, R 2007 *British Railway Station Architecture in Colour.* Hersham: Ian Allan

Holland, J 2013 *Dr Beeching's Axe – 50 Years On.* Newton Abbot: David & Charles

Hoole, K 1985 *Railway Stations of the North East.* Newton Abbot: David & Charles

Irving, R J 1969 *London's Termini.* Newton Abbot: David & Charles

Jackson, A A 1978 *London's Local Railways.* Newton Abbot: David & Charles

Jardine, N 2002 *British Railway Stations in Colour.* Hinckley: Midland Publishing

Leigh, C 1981 *GWR Country Stations.* Hersham: Ian Allan

Leigh, C 1984 *GWR Country Stations: 2.* Hersham: Ian Allan

Lloyd, D and Insall, D 1967 *Railway Station Architecture.* Newton Abbot: David & Charles

Meeks, C L V 1956 *The Railroad Station.* New Haven and London: Yale University Press

Minnis, J 1985 *Southern Country Stations: 2 – South Eastern and Chatham Railway.* Hersham: Ian Allan

Minnis, J 2011 *Britain's Lost Railways.* London: Aurum Press

Parissien, S 1997 *Station to Station.* London: Phaidon

Parissien, S and Holder, J (eds) 2004 *British Transport Architecture in the 20th Century.* New Haven and London: Yale University Press

Richards, J and MacKenzie, J M 1986 *The Railway Station.* Oxford: Oxford University Press

Simmons, J 1986 *The Railway in Town and Country.* Newton Abbot: David & Charles

Simmons, J 1991 *The Victorian Railway.* London: Thames & Hudson

Simmons, J and Biddle, G 1997 *The Oxford Companion to British Railway History.* Oxford: Oxford University Press

Thomas, D S J 2011 *The Country Railway.* London: Frances Lincoln

Vaughan, A 1997 *Railwaymen, Politics and Money.* London: John Murray

Vaughan, A 2010 *The Intemperate Engineer.* Shepperton: Ian Allan

Whishaw, F 1842 *The Railways of Great Britain and Ireland.* London: John Weale/Nabu Public Domain Reprints.

Wikeley, N and Middleton, J 1971 *Railway Stations – Southern Region.* Seaton: Peco Publications

Wolmar, C 2007 *Fire and Steam.* London: Atlantic

INDEX